WINE COUNTRY QUILTS

A BOUNTY OF FLAVORFUL PROJECTS FOR ANY PALETTE

PUBLISHING

Cyndy Lyle Rymer & Jennifer Rounds

©2002 by Cyndy Lyle Rymer and Jennifer Rounds

Editor-in-Chief: Darra Williamson

Development Editor/Technical Editor: Laura M. Reinstatler

Copyeditor/Proofreaders: Annette Bailey/Stacy Chamness

Design Director/Book and Cover Design: Kristen Yenche

Illustrator: Richard Sheppard

Photo Stylist: Diane Pedersen

Production Assistant: Kirstie L. McCormick

Photography: Sharon Risedorph, Amy Marson, Diane Pedersen, Cyndy Lyle Rymer

Front cover: *Road to California: Fair Play Fun* (page 27) by Cyndy Lyle Rymer, photo by Garry Gay. Many thanks to Barbara and Tom Allen for allowing us to photograph at Delta Diablo Vineyard.

Back cover: *Grape Wreath Medallion* by Nancy Busby, (page 14); *Above the Clouds* by Lynn Koolish (page 23).

Attention Teachers: C&T Publishing, Inc. encourages you to use this book as a text for teaching. Contact us at 800-284-1114 or www.ctpub.com for more information about the C&T Teachers Program.

We take great care to ensure that the information included in this book is accurate and presented in good faith, but no warranty is provided nor results guaranteed. Having no control over the choices of materials or procedures used, neither the author nor C&T Publishing, Inc. shall have any liability to any person or entity with respect to any loss or damage caused directly or indirectly by the information contained in this book. For your convenience, we post an up-to-date listing of corrections on our web page (www.ctpub.com). If a correction is not already noted, please contact our customer service department at ctinfo@ctpub.com or at PO Box 1456, Lafayette, CA 94549.

Trademarked (™) and Registered Trademark (®) names are used throughout this book. Rather than use the symbols with every occurrence of a trademark and registered trademark name, we are using the names only in the editorial fashion and to the benefit of the owner, with no intention of infringement.

Excerpt on page 7 from *Harvest of Joy, My Passion, My Life*, copyright © 1998 by Robert Mondavi, reprinted by permission of Harcourt, Inc.

Library of Congress Cataloging-in-Publication Data
Rymer, Cyndy Lyle.
   Wine country quilts : a bounty of flavorful projects for any palette / Cyndy Lyle Rymer and Jennifer Rounds.
      p. cm.
   ISBN 1-57120-203-X (Paper trade)
   1. Patchwork--Patterns. 2. Quilting--Patterns. 3. Wine in art. I. Rounds, Jennifer. II. Title.
   TT835 .R948 2003
   746.46'041--dc21
                                        2002154141

Printed in China

10 9 8 7 6 5 4 3 2 1

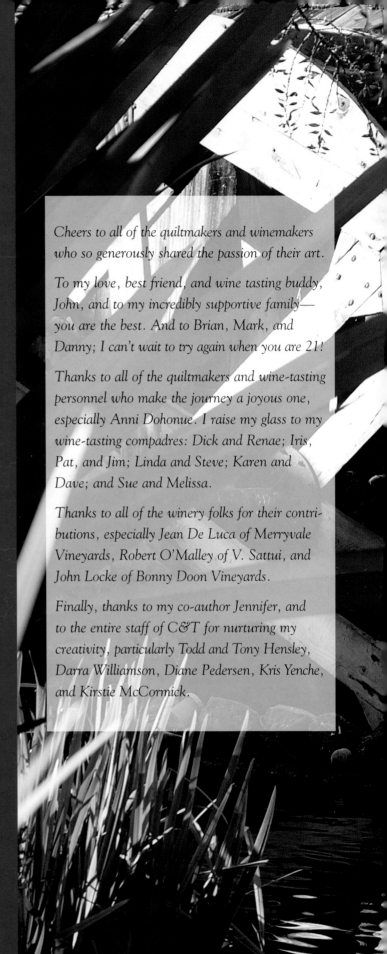

Cheers to all of the quiltmakers and winemakers who so generously shared the passion of their art.

To my love, best friend, and wine tasting buddy, John, and to my incredibly supportive family— you are the best. And to Brian, Mark, and Danny; I can't wait to try again when you are 21!

Thanks to all of the quiltmakers and wine-tasting personnel who make the journey a joyous one, especially Anni Dohonue. I raise my glass to my wine-tasting compadres: Dick and Renae; Iris, Pat, and Jim; Linda and Steve; Karen and Dave; and Sue and Melissa.

Thanks to all of the winery folks for their contributions, especially Jean De Luca of Merryvale Vineyards, Robert O'Malley of V. Sattui, and John Locke of Bonny Doon Vineyards.

Finally, thanks to my co-author Jennifer, and to the entire staff of C&T for nurturing my creativity, particularly Todd and Tony Hensley, Darra Williamson, Diane Pedersen, Kris Yenche, and Kirstie McCormick.

Contents

Shared Passions 4

Projects

Through the Grapevine 10
Grape Wreath Medallion 14
Above the Clouds 23
Road to California: Fair Play Fun 27
Pinot Noir 33
Emerald Valley 36
Grapes Nouveau 42
Colors of the Vineyard 46
In the Arbor 52
Private Collection 59
Wine Tasting with Friends 64
Puttin' on the Glitz Table Topper 67
Blind Wine-Tasting Bags 69
Post Wine-Tasting Dinner 70

Wine Country Memorabilia Projects

Shadow Boxes with a Twist 73
Cork Critters 74
A Classic Pairing: 74
Peanut Butter & Jelly

Quilting Basics 78

Directory of Quilt Shops and Wineries 80

Bibliography 94

Index 95

SHARED *PASSIONS*

Wine is sunlight held together by water. *Galileo*

Along the Silverado Trail, Napa Valley, Califor...

Inspiration comes at funny times. The idea for this book bubbled up like a glass of sparkling wine when I attended a quilting retreat a few years ago. I was intoxicated by the vision of combining two of my passions: quiltmaking and wine tasting.

Quilts and quilt books have been my pleasure and occupation for quite some time, while wine tasting is a recent hobby. Six years ago the trauma of a cross-country

Retzlaff Vineyard, Livermore Valley, California

move to California was eased when my husband John and I made friends with some avid wine enthusiasts. We are fortunate to live twenty minutes away from the Livermore Valley, and only an hour from Napa and Sonoma. Day trips and occasional blissful weekends are spent happily exploring more distant wine regions. I can think of no better way to celebrate two pursuits that bring me such joy than to create a book uniting the artistry of quilts with the splendor of the various wine regions of the United States.

Quilting and winemaking are both artful pursuits strongly rooted in tradition. In addition, as any quilter will tell you, the community spirit of quilters is strong and special. This spirit is also shared in winemaking, between the grape growers, the winemakers, and the tasting room staff.

There are handcrafted wines just as there are handcrafted quilts. The similarities are infinite: quilters and winemakers are passionate about their craft; both pursue self-expression and superior craftsmanship. As art and wine have long been intertwined, it is no wonder

that quilters create vineyard-related quilts of stunning beauty.

The quilts featured here represent individual attempts to capture the beauty of the vineyards, whether in the form of a landscape, a single cluster of grapes, or special memories from days roaming the back roads of wine country. Even if you never visit a winery, you can get a feel for the allure of the countryside represented in these quilts. Each region of the country has its own special places, and this book is meant to inspire you to translate your creative vision into quilts. Fabric—often embellished with thread, paint, beads, silk ribbon, yarns—just happens to be the medium most used by quilters in their pursuit of creative expression.

WINE COUNTRY VISTAS

Wine country is magical, romantic, sensual, and exemplifies the good life. Vineyards are incredibly beautiful at any time of year. In my travels through the hills and valleys of wine country, the seasonal colors of the vineyards have never failed to capture my imagination.

The picturesque sights stir my soul and spark my creativity. Vistas change according to the season. In early spring, the bright golden flowers of Napa Valley mustard grass dance among vibrant spring greenery. A couple months later, symmetrical rows of the first green shoots of the vines can be seen marching up a hillside behind a brick-red barn. In the summer, clusters of grapes appear beneath the vines that grow fuller and taller every day. Just before harvest, jewel-like blue, purple, red, and green grapes hang heavy on the vines. As the weather turns cooler, the vibrant green gives way to rusty reds and burnt oranges. In

Springtime in Napa Valley, California

the chill of winter, gnarly older vines are silhouetted against the deep blue dome of the sky, providing an eerie spectacle.

Within the vineyards, master gardeners (Wow! What a cool job!) plant a visual feast for the senses with colorful blooms juxtaposed against the green vines. Some wineries, such as Ferrari-Carano in Sonoma, are almost as well known for their fields of flowers as they are for their wine. Matanzas Creek in Sonoma is famous for its wine and for the softly waving fields of

lavender that greet you in the summer. Just south of Matanzas Creek is another winery with a dual claim to fame: B.R. Cohn is known for both its wines and estate-grown olive oil. Olive oil is becoming big business in the area. Sonoma held its first Olive Festival in 2002, and included contests for the best olive dishes and best wine to pair with olives.

EXPLORING A WINERY

For a quilter, architectural details of wine country such as windows, doors, iron gates, pergolas, garden sculptures, fountains, and fences provide ideas for future quilts.

Grasier Vineyards, near Calistoga, California

Winery architecture varies tremendously. Some of the older buildings date to pre-Prohibition days, and have been lovingly restored. Others range in style from nouveau-Mediterranean villas and sleek, ultramodern compounds, to unusual conversions of structures like hop kilns and small, unpretentious barns.

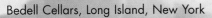
Bedell Cellars, Long Island, New York

Springtime in Napa Valley, California

INSIDE THE TASTING ROOM

Inside the wineries, details such as wine racks, the ever-present barrel stacks, or the textures, colors, and patterns of tasting room counters provide ideas that may be stashed away for future quilts. The sights, sounds, smells, and people you meet all add up to make wine tasting such memorable experiences. Winery owners must run a careful "personality profile" when hiring their staff. Most tasting room personnel are cheerful, well-informed, open to the most outrageous questions, and just plain fun to talk to.

We have encountered many natural storytellers working behind the counters, or running operations behind the scenes.

It's amusing to hear the words that describe the experience. When you walk into a barrel room, a distinctive yeasty-musty smell hits you full in the face. At crush time in the fall, the fresh-squeezed grape juice can smell stemmy and leafy, as well as fruity. I'm constantly learning new and unique adjectives to describe what I'm smelling or tasting. While quilters take classes to learn new techniques, there are many classes at wineries to educate the public about winemaking. Copia: The American Center for Wine, Food, and the Arts in downtown Napa is an entire complex dedicated to educating the public about all things wine related. It includes a restaurant, wine-tasting bar, garden, art galleries, classrooms, and much more.

Randall Graham, philosopher/winemaker of Bonny Doon Vineyards, California
photo by Alex Krause

THE BEST DAYS ON THE ROAD

My favorite days are those spent combining my pleasures: fabric shop hopping and wine-tasting. On one such trip, a tasting room pourer put me at ease forever by explaining that you need to know just one thing when tasting wine: It's either yummy or yucky. How simple! This enabled me, with my limited knowledge of wine, to enjoy any tasting room experience.

A similar thing can be said about quilts. You can be at a quilt show, a guild meeting during show-and-tell, or visiting a friend who shares a quilt made years ago by a relative: you either like the quilt or you don't. It's all a matter of personal preference. Some people prefer traditional quilts, while others like more abstract, contemporary forms of quilting. Some people prefer Pinot Noir, others like Zinfandel. I always thought I was strictly a white wine drinker, but now, when pasta with red sauce is put in front of me, pass the hearty spaghetti red!

Along the Silverado Trail, Napa, California

Robert Mondavi, the dean of California winemaking, so aptly stated, "Making good wine is a skill; making fine wine is an art.... Living a fine life is an art form. And learning this art requires time and patience and passion, and I believe that learning the art of life also requires a heart that is not constricted by fears or prejudices but is open and accepting and filled with compassion."

Quilters can relate to what Mr. Mondavi has to say. Our craft takes great patience and creativity, but it gives back so much in return. The goal of many quiltmakers is to capture a moment of inspiration in fabric, or to tell a personal story, and inspire others. The source of that inspiration varies. The works

of the contributing quilters represent a wide variety of wine regions throughout the country, and they all share a love for their natural surroundings.

INSIDE WINE COUNTRY QUILTS: A PASSPORT TO QUILTING ADVENTURES

Escape! We all feel the need now and then, especially in these high-stress times. There are so many gorgeous vineyards, and some of them just happen to be near quilt stores. Grab a friend or two or three (including a designated driver), pack a picnic, and try some of the wineries and quilt shops suggested on pages 80–93. See how many fabrics you can find that remind you of your day. One friend collected over twenty grape prints and coordinating fabrics in a very short period. Her quilt, *Through the Grapevine*, is on page 10.

You don't have to be a wine drinker to make the quilts and

View from Fitzpatrick Winery & Lodge, Fair Play, California

other projects. In quilts such as *Through the Grapevine* (page 10), *Road to California: Fair Play Fun* (page 27), or *Grapes Nouveau* (page 42), you can easily replace the grape print with a different print, such as a floral.

If you do enjoy wine and your friends' company, host a wine tasting party at home, followed by a potluck dinner—pages 70–71 are full of ideas and recipes for you.

Get your kids involved making the cork critters on page 74; with a lot of imagination and a little supervision they'll have a blast. Young sewers can try making the *Classic Pairing* quilt on page 74.

The Directory of Quilt Shops and Wineries presents a taste of *some* of the major wine-producing states. If you are planning a visit, you can stop at both wineries and quilt shops along the way. Bring a camera to record all the incredible sights along the way!

Stuart Cellars, Temecula Valley, California, *photo by Stephen Eldred*

SOUTH OF MONTEREY

If you have just finished a class at the fabulous Empty Spools Seminars in Asilomar, or are anywhere near Monterey, plan to spend some time exploring the nearby quilt shops in Pacific Grove: Back Porch and the Hand Maden. In downtown Monterey, on Cannery Row, look for a mega-tasting room with an incredible view of the Pacific Ocean: A Taste of Monterey, where you can sample wines from 35 different Monterey wineries. Then slowly head south to one of the prettiest drives in California: Carmel Valley Road. Here you will find Chateau Julien Wine Estate (great for picnicking), Bernardus Winery and Vineyard, Galante Vineyard (call ahead for an appointment), Joullian Vineyards, Heller Estate/Durney Vineyards (with sculptures by Toby Heller), and Robert Talbott Vineyards, all within or close to the extremely charming Carmel Valley Village. If you are due for a special treat, spend a night or two at the Bernardus Lodge, which offers a variety of spa treatments, a gourmet restaurant, and of course, wines from the Bernardus Winery.

Jewels in the Vineyard at Dawn, 39" x 46",
Mary Ellen Parsons, Carmel Valley, CA, 2002.

Mary Ellen and her husband Bill own and operate the Parsonage Village Vineyard and Parsonage Winery (no tasting room yet) in Carmel Valley, California. Mary Ellen's studio is located in the midst of the vineyard, providing her with lots of inspiration. She loves using her Fiskar "snips" to harvest grapes, but is dreading the day Bill follows through on his plan to purchase miner's helmets so he can realize his goal of harvesting grapes in the dark.

California Colors, 31" x 39",
Mary Ellen Parsons, Carmel Valley, CA, 2001.
From the collection of Marilyn Beach

California Colors decorates the Parsonage label for vintage 2000, the first harvest. A portion of *Jewels in the Vineyard at Dawn* was used for the 2001 label. Mary Ellen will happily continue creating vineyard quilts for each year because she knows where her fabric money is coming from.

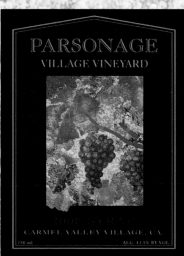

Retzlaff Winery, Livermore Valley, California

LIVERMORE VALLEY

Traveling to San Francisco? You're in our neck of the woods, and you should add the East Bay and Livermore Valley quilt stores and wineries to your list of places to visit (see page 82). It is interesting to note that at one point the wineries here outnumbered those in Napa. They range from the posh Wente Vineyards, site of spectacular summer concerts, a golf course, and a wonderful restaurant, to the more rural-feeling, extremely fun Livermore Valley Cellars. Be sure to stop by Fenestra Winery and say hello to Fran Replogle, a fellow quilter who also happens to offer great recipes in her newsletter.

Three years ago on a blistering hot Labor Day my husband and I joined forces with new wine-tasting friends and enjoyed the Livermore Valley vineyards' annual two-day open house. An extremely well-organized bus system delivers you to several wineries in one day. The number of people braving the heat to sample the wines, delicious culinary treats, and live music was astounding.

Through the Grapevine

Finished Quilt Size: 84" x 105" (queen size)
Finished block size: Grapevine Variation 12½" square
Machine pieced by Joyce Engels Lytle, San Ramon, California, machine quilted by Linda Leathersich

At the time this book was under discussion, Joyce participated in a four-day marathon "shop hop" sponsored by several San Francisco Bay area quilt stores. She collected 26 different grape or wine-motif fabrics, usually one-yard lengths. Joyce said it was fun to go from shop to shop looking for one particular style of fabric or color range. For the quilt above, she used six of the fabrics collected.

A tip for shop-hoppers: Take a swatch of each fabric and identify it with the shop where it was purchased in case more yardage is needed for a future quilt project.

FABRIC REQUIREMENTS

Dark purple: 1⅛ yards for blocks and inner border

Green grape print: 2¾ yards for blocks and binding

Purple grape print: 1¾ yards for blocks

Beige background grape print: 2⅓ yards for blocks

Green stripe: ¾ yard for second border

Multicolor: ⅜ yard for accent border

Green plaid: 2¾ yards for outer border

Backing: 7⅓ yards

Batting: 88" x 109"

Threads to match

CUTTING

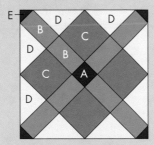

Grapevine Variation Block

Note: All strips are cut by the width of the fabric, usually 42".

Center (A) squares and (E) triangles: Cut 7 strips 2¼" wide, then cut the strips into 105 squares 2¼". Set aside 35 squares for the center A squares. Cut the remaining 70 squares diagonally once to make 140 E triangles.

Trellis (B) rectangles: Cut 17 strips 4" wide, then cut the strips into 280 rectangles 2¼" x 4".

Grape (C) squares: Cut 14 strips 4" wide, then cut the strips into 140 squares 4".

Side (D) triangles: Cut 12 strips 6¼" wide, then cut the strips into 70 squares 6¼". Cut the squares diagonally twice to make 280 D triangles.

Inner border: Cut 9 strips 2¼" wide. Sew the strips together end to end with diagonal seams. From this strip, cut two 88" lengths for the side borders and two 66½" lengths for the top and bottom borders.

Stripe border: Cut 9 strips 2½" wide. Sew strips together end to end. From this strip, cut two 91½" lengths for the side borders and two 70½" lengths for the top and bottom borders.

Accent border: Cut 9 strips 1" wide. Sew the strips together end to end with diagonal seams. From this strip, cut two 95½" lengths for the side borders and two 70½" lengths for the top and bottom borders.

Outer border: This border is cut on the lengthwise grain. Cut 2 strips 7½" x 95½" for the side borders and 2 strips 5½" x 84½" for the top and bottom borders.

Binding: Cut 10 strips 2¼" wide. Sew strips together diagonally into one length.

BLOCK ASSEMBLY

1. Sew the inner block together as shown. Press as indicated. The block should measure 9¼" x 9¼".

Make one per block.

2. Sew the side units together as shown. Press as indicated.

Make 4 per block.

3. Sew the 4 side units to the inner block. Press the seams toward the side units. The blocks should measure 13" square. Trim as necessary, allowing a ¼" seam allowance. Repeat steps 1–3 for a total of 35 blocks.

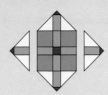

QUILT ASSEMBLY

1. Sew the blocks together in 7 rows of 5 blocks. Press the seams open.

2. Sew the rows together. Press the seams open.

3. Sew the inner purple border sides to the quilt first, then the top and bottom borders. Press the seams toward the border.

4. Sew the stripe border sides first, then the top and bottom borders. Press the seams toward the inner purple border.

5. Using a ½" seam allowance, sew the accent border sides first, then the top and bottom borders. Press the seams toward the accent border. Once the outer border is sewn on, the accent border will be an accurate ¼" wide.

6. Using a ¼" seam allowance, sew the outer border sides first, then the top and bottom borders. Press the seams toward the outer border.

FINISHING

Refer to the Quilting Basics on pages 78–79.

1. Press, then trim the corners and edges to square up the quilt top.

2. Layer the quilt top, batting, and backing. Pin or thread baste.

3. Quilt as desired. A vineyard theme with a variety of grapes, vines, and leaves is appropriate here.

4. Bind or finish the quilt as desired.

5. Attach a hanging sleeve and label to the back of the quilt.

Bruno by Darcie Kent, reproduced courtesy of Livermore Valley Winegrower's Association and Darcie Kent

Quilt Assembly Diagram

Flowers for Mommie, 28" x 42", Vicki Chambers, Napa Valley, CA, 1999.

This quilt, started in a workshop taught by Ruth McDowell, is Vicki's rendition of her daughters running through the brilliant yellow mustard that grows during spring in their vineyard.

Got a Lot of Sunshine in My Heart (left), 15½" x 33", Anni Donohue, Napa Valley, CA, 2001. Machine pieced and appliquéd

This quilt was created for a challenge by Quiltmaker, a quilt store in Napa. Contestants were provided with two fabrics representing the grapes and mustard of the Napa Valley, and permitted to add only three other fabrics. This quilt represents the sun over the vineyards and was inspired by the challenge fabric and the wonderful valley Anni calls home.

Stella de Uva (right), 26" x 33", Tam Ravenhill, Napa Valley, CA, 2001. Machine pieced and appliquéd, hand quilted

Spurred on by the Persian Star block in *Wedgeworks* by Cheryl Phillips, *Stella de Uva*, or Star of Grapes, is a wine label from the NapaValley, Tam's home, and a place where the grapes are as inspiring as the stars above.

TRAVELING IN NAPA VALLEY, CALIFORNIA

Trying to visit the many Napa wineries in one trip can be a daunting task. One way to tackle the trip is to do the wineries along Route 29 for one or two days, then wind your way along the less-traveled Silverado Trail on a separate day. For an overview of the winemaking process, start at a winery that offers a tour; Mondavi and Beringer are both good candidates.

To escape to a magical world, start your day at the di Rosa Preserve, site of a winery-turned-residence and home to a private collection of more than 1800 works of art. The site also boasts 200 acres of meadows, gardens, and a 35-acre lake. Reservations are required.

Another good starting point for quilters is the Quiltmaker Shop in downtown Napa; look for the purple wall.

You'll run out of time before you run out of options. There are great picnic sites at many of the wineries, as well as restaurants, B&Bs, spas, art galleries, and hiking trails. Treat yourself to a birds'-eye view of Napa from a hot air balloon. For a completely different experience, head north to Calistoga, and indulge in a mud bath. Funky, but relaxing!

Folie à Deux

1998
Napa Valley

Cabernet Sauvignon

Grape Wreath
Medallion

Finished Quilt Size: 50" x 50"

Designed, appliquéd, trapuntoed, and hand quilted by Nancy Busby, Rio Vista, California. Photo taken at V. Sattui Winery

Nancy Busby, an expert appliqué artist and teacher at the Cotton Patch Quilt Shop in Lafayette, California, designed this quilt as a teaching tool for a variety of techniques, such as appliqué, trapunto, and quilting. Appliqué will always be her first love, but Nancy continues to explore all types of hand and machine piecing and quilting.

FABRIC REQUIREMENTS

Center square and Trapunto border: 2¼ yards white

Grapes: ⅛ yard each of 3 or 4 different shades of one color

Leaves and stems: ⅛ yard each of 4 shades of green

First and third borders: 1 yard green print

Trapunto backing fabric: 1½ yards of a loosely woven neutral

Backing: 3⅛ yards

Batting: 1 yard of 60"-wide high-loft for trapunto

Batting: 54" x 54" (Cotton/polyester batting is recommended for machine quilting; it helps to hold the layers together.)

Binding: ½ yard

¾" appliqué pins

Needles: #11 sharps for appliqué, #10 sharps for hand sewing, yarn needle

Threads to match background fabric

Green embroidery floss or #12 perle cotton to match satin-stitched leaves

Thread-Fuse or Stitch 'n Fuse for satin-stitch appliqué (optional)

Wash-Away basting thread

Invisible nylon thread

Freezer paper

Water-soluble glue stick

Natural-colored 4-ply yarn for trapunto vines and grapes

#2 or #3 pencil, Berol silver pencil

Plastic circle template in multiple sizes (available in office supply stores)

File folders for templates

CUTTING

Note: Nancy recommends prewashing all fabrics.

Center square: Cut 1 square 24½" x 24½".

First border: Cut 2 strips 2½" x 24½"; cut 2 strips 2½" x 28½".

Trapunto border: Cut 5 strips 9½" x width of fabric.

Third border: Cut 5 strips 2½" x width of fabric. Sew the strips together end to end with diagonal seams. From this strip, cut two 46½" lengths and two 50½" lengths.

Binding: Cut 6 strips 2½" x width of fabric.

CENTER MEDALLION

Lightly finger-press the 24½" square in quarters to locate the center. Make a grape wreath medallion master pattern using the leaf pattern on page 18 and the plastic circle template in multiple sizes for the grape clusters. Place it onto a light source such as a lightbox or window. Lightly trace the pattern onto the square, marking the center of the

grapes with a dot rather than tracing the whole grape.

GRAPE LEAF WREATH

1. Trace each leaf and stem from your master pattern onto the dull side of freezer paper. Carefully cut out all freezer paper patterns on the drawn lines; all edges should be smooth.

2. Use the plastic circle template to create grape templates ranging in size from ¾"–1", drawing them onto file folders. Carefully cut the templates from the file folders.

Blanket-Stitched Leaves and Stems

For the 9 machine-appliquéd leaves and stems, use a hot, dry iron to press the freezer paper templates—shiny side down—onto the wrong side of the green fabrics. Leave at least 1½" space around these leaves.

Cut out the leaves, adding a ½" seam allowance.

Thread your sewing machine with Stitch 'n Fuse in the bobbin and thread to match the fabric in the needle.

Set your machine for a smaller than normal stitch length, and stitch around the edge of the template on the right side of the fabric.

Trim the excess fabric, leaving a scant ⅛" seam allowance. You will trim this later as you stitch the leaf or stem to the center square.

Position the leaf on the background, and use a hot, dry iron to fuse the leaf to the center square.

Satin stitch the leaf and stem in place.

Needle-turned and Topstitched Leaves

1. From the green fabrics, cut out the 3 leaves to be needle-turned or topstitched, adding a ⅛" seam allowance.

2. Clip the curves and V's just before appliquéing onto the background.

3. Position each leaf on the center square, and appliqué in place.

GRAPES

1. Cut out the grapes, adding a ⅛" seam allowance to each.

2. Knot the end of a length of thread, and sew a line of gathering stitches ⅛" away from the traced line.

Tip: Start by taking one stitch, then backstitching, to prevent the gathering stitches from pulling out.

3. Place the cardboard circle templates on the back of the fabric circles. Pull the gathering thread tight so the fabric circles gather around the cardboard shapes. Tie off the gathering threads securely. Steam-press both sides of the circles with a hot iron.

4. Just before appliquéing each grape onto the center square, carefully clip the gathering thread and remove the cardboard shape.

5. Pat the gathers into place and apply a small dab of water-soluble glue to the wrong side of the grape to anchor it in position.

6. Position each grape on the center square and appliqué in place using a blind stitch.

TRAPUNTO BORDER

1. Sew the 9½" border strips end to end with diagonal seams. Cut 2 strips 9½" x 28½" for the top and bottom borders, and 2 strips 9½" x 46½" for the side borders.

2. Make a master pattern using patterns on page 19. Secure to a hard surface.

3. Fold the appropriate border piece in half crosswise and finger-press. Place the fold on the pattern center mark and tape the fabric in place over the pattern. Using a pencil, lightly trace the pattern onto the shorter top and bottom borders first. Use the circle template to carefully trace the grape clusters.

4. Repeat the process for the longer side borders. Line up the pattern and fabric centers.

5. Trace the corner pattern to both ends of the top and bottom borders. The grape clusters should hang toward the outside.

Hand-Stitched Grapes and Tendrils

1. Cut pieces of trapunto backing fabric large enough to cover each grape cluster and tendril.

2. Work with one cluster at a time. Place the backing fabric on the wrong side of the trapunto border behind the traced grape cluster. Position the border on a hard, flat surface and baste the backing fabric in place.

3. Thread a #10 sharps needle with sewing thread and knot the end. Bring the needle up from the back and use a back stitch to outline each grape. Return the needle to the back and end with a back stitch.

Note: Do not backstitch the area where the leaf overlaps the grapes.

4. Use the same process to outline the tendrils. To keep the dimensional look where the tendril crosses over itself, stitch so the tendril curls in one direction only. Pass the needle and thread under this area when coming back from the opposite direction.

5. Complete all outline stitching before "stuffing" the grapes or tendrils. To stuff, thread a yarn needle with 15"–18" of the natural-colored yarn. Working from the back of the piece, starting at one side of a grape, insert the needle into the backing fabric within the outlined area. Insert the needle between the two layers of fabric and out the opposite side. Pull the yarn through, leaving a short tail on the starting side. *Do not cut the yarn*. Re-insert the needle into the backing fabric next to the previous exit point and again run the needle between the two layers of fabric, bringing the needle out to the first entrance point. Repeat until the grape shape is filled with yarn. Do not overfill.

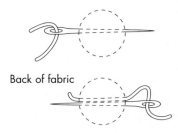

Insert the needle between fabric layers.

To fill the tendrils, split the yarn into plies and use only one-ply. Pass the yarn in one direction through the "tunnel" created by the outline stitches and under the tunnel coming from the opposite direction.

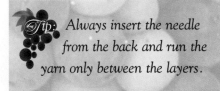

Tip: *Always insert the needle from the back and run the yarn only between the layers.*

Machine-Stitched Grape Leaves and Stems

1. Cut one strip of batting 9" x 28" for each border. You will stitch the corners separately.

2. Pin a batting strip to the back of each border strip. Pin around a leaf or stem as you get ready to stitch around each.

3. Thread your machine with regular sewing thread in the bobbin and Wash Away basting thread in the needle. Drop or cover the feed dogs and attach an open-toed embroidery or darning foot to stitch along the traced outlines. Loosen the top tension of your machine if necessary.

4. Trim the batting from around the stitched shapes, leaving ¼" of batting outside the stitched lines.

5. Complete all of the trapunto on the top and bottom borders first, then the side borders. Sew the border strips together at the corners; you will end up with what looks like a square donut. Leave the seam allowance free at the inner corners. Complete the trapunto in the corners.

QUILT ASSEMBLY

Refer to Borders on page 78.

1. Sew the green print top and bottom first borders, then the side borders to the appliquéd center square medallion.

2. Carefully pin the trapunto "donut" border onto the quilt top, one side at a time. It helps to sew one side, then the opposite side. This makes it easier to attach the remaining sides.

3. Press all seams toward the first border.

4. Sew the green print top and bottom third borders, then the side outer borders to the quilt top.

Quilt Assembly Diagram

Sutter Home Inn, Napa Valley, California

FINISHING

Refer to Quilting Basics on pages 78–79.

1. Mark for quilting as desired. (There is no need to mark meander quilting.)

2. Layer the backing, batting, and quilt top. Baste. Pin basting is recommended for machine quilting.

3. Start quilting the center square of the quilt top. If you are machine quilting, drop or cover the feed dogs, and use a darning foot or open-toe embroidery foot. Use thread to match the backing in the bobbin, and invisible nylon thread in the needle.

4. Stitch around the grapes and stems, following the outline stitches you completed for the trapunto. Machine stitch the veins on the leaves.

5. Machine quilt the first border using matching thread.

6. Quilt the area between the first border and the trapunto design of the second border.

7. Continue at the outside edge of the trapunto border. Move to the grape clusters and quilt in this area also.

8. Tie off and bury the ends of any loose threads between the quilt layers.

9. Square up the quilt. Machine baste around the perimeter of the quilt, staying within the ¼" seam allowance.

10. Bind or finish the quilt as desired.

11. Attach a hanging sleeve and label to the back of the quilt.

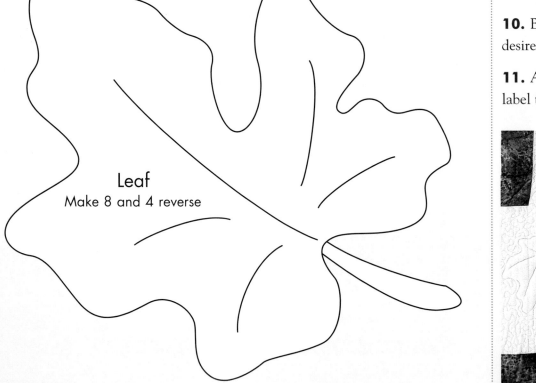

Leaf
Make 8 and 4 reverse

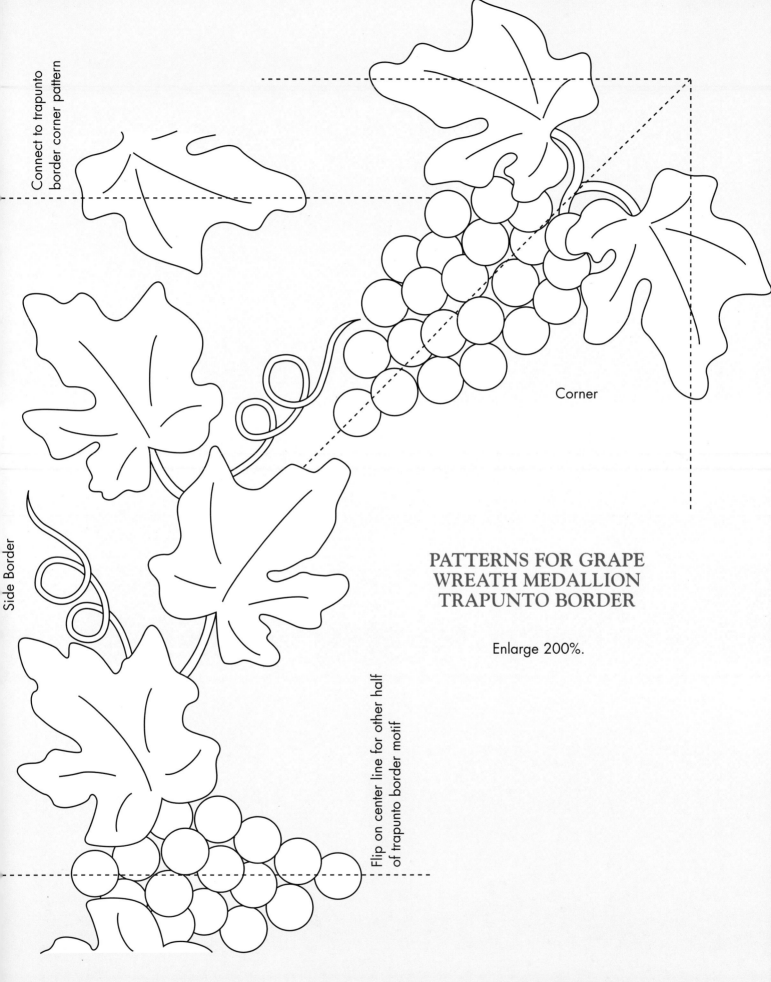

Corner

PATTERNS FOR GRAPE WREATH MEDALLION TRAPUNTO BORDER

Enlarge 200%.

Side Border

Flip on center line for other half of trapunto border motif

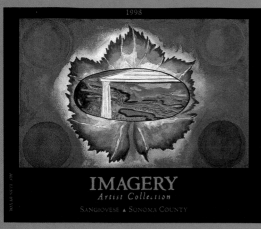

Original artwork by Gregory Amenoff

WINE LABELS AS ART

We can't go into any store that sells wine without getting totally absorbed by a hunt for the best labels. Many wineries have realized that labels are a natural way to display art, making them a great collector's item. Labels also help sell wine and establish a winery's identity. Surfing the web for wineries that use artistic labels on their bottles can be a source of inspiration for small quilts.

Several wineries encourage contemporary artists to create works of art to be used on wine labels; some, such as Messina Hof in Bryan, Texas, sponsor an annual artist's competition for new vintage labels. Other wineries are to be applauded for encouragement of local artists; these include (but are not limited to) Imagery Estate Winery in Sonoma, California; Justin Vineyards near Paso Robles, California; Les Bourgeois Vineyards in Rocheport, Missouri; Truro Vineyards of Cape Cod, Massachusetts; Cascata Winery, Watkins Glen, New York; and Good Harbor Vineyards in Lake Leelenau, Michigan.

Flora Springs Label Quilt, 14" x 14", Catherine Comyns, Walnut Creek, CA, 2002. Hand appliquéd and quilted.

Lighthouse Golden Autumn *by Lois Griffel*

20

Les Bourgeois Label Quilt, 14" x 14", Cyndy Lyle Rymer, Danville, CA, 2002. Machine appliquéd and quilted.

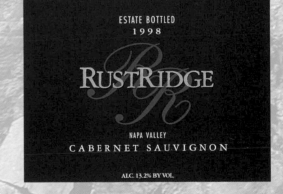

ESTATE BOTTLED
1998

RUSTRIDGE

NAPA VALLEY

CABERNET SAUVIGNON

ALC. 13.2% BY VOL.

Rust Ridge Label Quilt, 17" x 15", Anni Donohue, Napa, CA, 2002. Machine appliquéd and hand quilted.

Original artwork by Bob Nugent

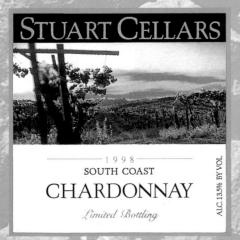

STUART CELLARS

1998
SOUTH COAST
CHARDONNAY
Limited Bottling

ALC. 13.5% BY VOL

BENZIGER
IMAGERY

1994
ZINFANDEL
PORT
DRY CREEK

BLACK
SHEEP
SIERRA FOOTHILLS
AMADOR COUNTY
ZINFANDEL
1998

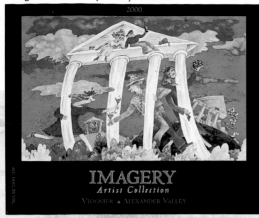

Original artwork by Gladys Nilsson

Original artwork by Pam Findleton

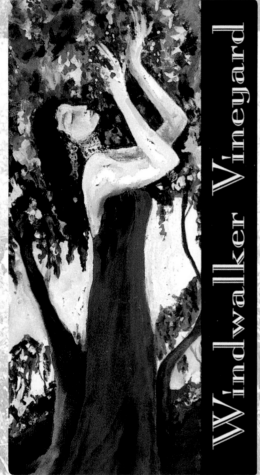

Serendipitous Vineyard, 41" x 32½", Cyndy Lyle Rymer, Danville, CA, 2002. Machine pieced and quilted

My subconscious was definitely at work in the design of this quilt. In a workshop with Caryl Bryer Fallert, we were required to create 60 doodles. When it dawned on me that one of the doodles resembled a vineyard, I knew I had my design. Caryl's graduated flying geese design reminds me of the birds who love the grapes that grow in my backyard.

Beautiful Mustard, 39" x 31", Vicki Chambers, Napa Valley, CA, 1999.

Vicki lives in the midst of a beautiful vineyard in the famous Stag's Leap district of Napa Valley. Vicki was inspired by the artwork of Jessel Miller, a Napa artist known for her colorful Mustard Festival posters and children's books.

Above the Clouds

Finished Quilt Size: 34" x 48"

Machine appliquéd and quilted by Lynn Koolish, Berkeley, California

Above the Clouds is a quilted interpretation of a watercolor painting of the same name by Healdsburg resident and artist Richard Sheppard. No piecing is required! The "puzzle pieces" of the quilt are cut out using freezer-paper templates and placed on a muslin foundation "map." The raw fabric edges are covered with fusible bias tape.

Above the Clouds original watercolor by Richard Sheppard

HEAD TO HEALDSBURG

In northern California, just west of Sonoma, the town of Healdsburg has become a happening place with a variety of incredible restaurants, chic boutiques, and galleries. There is a wonderful quilt store (Fabrications), and you can stop by Plaza Arts and Gallery to see more of Richard Sheppard's watercolors. However, it's the outlying area that is the real draw. The flavor of the wineries runs from small and intimate, such as Hop Kiln or Joseph Swan Vineyards, to the grandness of Chateau Souverain, or the more modern style of Clos du Bois. A leisurely drive along Westside Road is a treat for the senses. The Russian River offers opportunities for canoeing, kayaking, or tubing. Tempted to stay the night (and who wouldn't be)? There are plenty of B&Bs and hotels to choose from. Drive even farther north to Jimtown, and you'll find the general mercantile Jimtown Store, described as a "clubhouse for the community," and just a fun place to visit.

FABRIC REQUIREMENTS

Balloons

Yellow: ⅛ yard

Yellow-orange: ¼ yard

Warm red (flame red): ⅛ yard

Cool red (fuchsia): ¼ yard

Bright green: ⅛ yard

Purple: ¼ yard

Sky and Clouds

Turquoise blues (ranging from dark to light): 1 yard total

White-on-white: ½ yard

Hills and Leaves

Greens (ranging from yellow-green, green, and blue-green): 1 yard total

Grapes

Variegated purples: ½ yard total

Inner border: ¼ yard bright green

Outer border: ½ yard each blue (for top section) and variegated dark green (for bottom section; can be the same fabric as the bottom section of hills)

Foundation: 1½ yards muslin

Backing: 1½ yards

Binding: ½ yard

Pre-made ¼" black fusible bias tape: 2–3 packages, or 22–33 yards of black bias tape (the exact amount needed depends on the method used when making the grapes)

Threads to match fabrics

Fabric glue

Freezer paper

Masking tape

¼" Steam-a-Seam2 fusible tape (if not using pre-made fusible bias tape)

Sharpie fine point permanent pen

Pencil

CUTTING

Inner border: Cut 4 strips ⅞" x width of fabric.

Outer border: Cut 3 strips 4" x width of fabric from the blue fabric and 3 strips 4" x width of fabric from the dark green fabric.

QUILT ASSEMBLY

1. Enlarge the pattern on page 26 785%. (A copy center may need to enlarge it in several steps.)

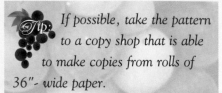

Tip: *If possible, take the pattern to a copy shop that is able to make copies from rolls of 36"- wide paper.*

2. Tape or iron sheets of freezer paper together to make a 36" x 52" rectangle. If you are using masking tape, place tape on the **dull** side of the freezer paper.

3. Tape the master pattern to a light box or large window. Trace the enlarged pattern onto the **shiny** side of the freezer paper with a Sharpie pen. On the **dull** side of the freezer paper, use a pencil to indicate the color to use for each piece of the design. If you are using directional fabrics (with a stripe or other distinctive pattern), you may also want to make notes about the direction in which the piece will be used so you can more easily align the fabric.

Tip: *If you don't want to make separate templates for each grape, or group of grapes, use the lines on the pattern to make a complete green background. Then make the grapes using the method of your choice: appliquéd yo-yos, fused circles, grapes stuffed with batting, or a variety of buttons or beads.*

4. Lay the muslin foundation fabric on top of the shiny side of the freezer paper. Using the Sharpie marker, trace the design onto the muslin; this is your map for the placement of each fabric piece. Set the muslin aside.

5. Work in sections to cut the freezer paper templates apart. Iron each template onto the **wrong** side of the selected fabrics. Cut out the fabric pieces along the edges of the freezer paper. Leave the freezer paper on for now.

6. Pin the fabric pieces into place on the muslin foundation. When you have all the fabric cut out and placed, step back and check to see if the fabrics are aesthetically pleasing.

Tip: *If there are any pieces you are not happy with, peel off the freezer paper and try another fabric. (The freezer paper can be peeled off and re-ironed a number of times.)*

7. When you are pleased with your fabric selections, peel off the freezer paper and place the pieces exactly so the edges butt up against each other. There should be very little space between the pieces. Use a bit of glue along all the edges to tack each piece onto the muslin foundation.

8. When all the edges are glued down, you are ready to apply the bias tape to cover the raw fabric edges.

Note: If you have made your own bias tape you need to add the ¼" Steam-A-Seam2 fusible adhesive to the wrong side of the bias strips. Follow the manufacturer's instructions.

9. Study the design to plan placement of the fusible bias. Plan ahead and note which strip of fusible bias can cover the cut ends of other pieces of the fusible bias tape. For example, if you fuse the diagonal lines on the upper hillside first, the horizontal strips will cover the cut edges.

Note: Do not heat-set the tape in place until all of the raw edges have been covered.

Tip: *Trim the cut edges of the bias tape so they match the angles of any crossing pieces.*

Plan ahead so that the cut ends of the bias tape are covered.

10. Work slowly and make sure the bias tape is covering all the raw edges before ironing, then fuse the bias tape onto the design following the manufacturer's instructions.

Tip: *For sharper curves, pull the bias tape just a little to help ease it around the curves. Hold the iron in place long enough to make sure the bias tape is securely fused. To make the sharp points of the leaves and clouds, take a tuck or make a miter in the bias tape as needed to fit the shape.*

Make a tuck or miter to form a point in the bias tape

11. After the bias tape is fused, topstitch both sides to hold it securely in place. This can be done in sections as the tape is fused on, or you can fuse all the bias tape, then topstitch.

Tip: *If you have a double needle that is the correct size for your bias tape, you can use it for most of the topstitching. For the clouds and the grape leaves, you'll need to use a single needle and sew each side of the bias tape separately.*

If the grapes have not already been added, do so now.

Give the quilt a final pressing and trim it so the edges are straight and the corners are square.

BORDERS

Refer to Borders on page 78.

Sew the ⅞"-wide inner border strips together end to end with diagonal seams. Measure and cut the borders as described in Quilting Basics on page 78. Sew the side inner borders to the quilt top, then add the top and bottom borders.

To extend the curve of the hills into each side border as the quilter did, place a 4"-wide dark green border strip next to the quilt top on each side. Overlap a 4"-wide blue border strip where the hills meet the sky. Lap the end of the blue border over the end of the dark green border, allowing enough overlap to accommodate your chosen angle. With a pencil, lightly draw a line continuing the curvature of the hills onto the blue strip and use a rotary cutter to cut on this line, through both layers. Sew the

ends together using a ⅛" seam allowance. Sew the outer border to the side of the quilt matching hill/sky seams with the seams on the quilt. Repeat for the second side border.

Measure, cut, and sew the 4"-wide blue top border and 4"-wide dark green bottom border to the quilt.

FINISHING

Refer to the Quilting Basics on pages 78–79.

1. Press, then trim the corners and edges to square up the quilt top.

2. Layer the quilt top, batting, and backing. Baste.

3. Outline-quilt the major shapes to anchor the quilt top, then quilt each area of the quilt with a pattern that relates to the quilt's design. For example, quilt the clouds with cloud shapes and the sky with curvy lines that suggest air currents. Quilt grape leaves in the bottom portion of the quilt and extending into the border.

4. Bind or finish the quilt as desired.

5. Attach a hanging sleeve and label to the back of the quilt.

Master Pattern

Road to California: Fair Play Fun

Finished Quilt Size: 47½" x 56½"

Finished Block Size: 9" x 9"

Machine pieced and appliquéd by Cyndy Lyle Rymer, Danville, California;
machine quilted by Kathy Sandbach, Bandon, Oregon

This quilt celebrates a fondness for my adopted home state. I had already purchased the fabrics, but wasn't quite sure how I would use them. A glance through my first quilting book, Ruby McKim's *101 Patchwork Patterns*, turned up a block called Road to California. I was off and stitching. The quilt also recognizes my roots: Brian Fitzpatrick (winemaker at Fitzpatrick Winery), my husband, and I all grew up in the same county in New Jersey. Small world! As a nod to our Celtic heritage, I added the machine-appliquéd "S" design to the border, along with small hand-painted purple flowers. Wherever you find a winery there are bound to be flowers!

WINES WITH AN ALTITUDE

Fair Play, which is slightly northeast of Sacramento, is one of the newest appellations in California. Wineries such as Windwalker Vineyards, Perry Creek Vineyard, Fleur de Lys Winery, and Boeger Winery, are smaller, and extremely friendly. The Fitzpatrick Winery and Lodge offers a Ploughman's Lunch (cheese, bread, fruit), and on a beautiful day there is nothing better than sitting on the patio and taking in the spectacular views. Spend a night or two in their wonderful rooms; plan to bring a bathing suit for the hot tub and pool, which present the same incredible views. On Friday nights during the summer, Diane and Brian Fitzpatrick make delicious wood-fired pizzas. Book a room early for these special nights—they fill quickly.

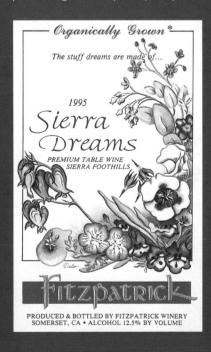

FABRIC REQUIREMENTS

Grape print: 1 yard for blocks and third border (cut crosswise, or 2 yards for borders cut lengthwise)

Light violet: ⅔ yard

Light green: ½ yard

Two-toned burgundy/green print: ½ yard

Dark green: ¼ yard for first border

Red-violet: 1⅜ yards for second border (cut lengthwise, or ⅔ yard for borders cut crosswise)

Green: ¾ yard for vines

White or light purple: ¼ yard for flowers

Binding: ½ yard

Backing: 3 yards

Batting: 52" x 61"

¼" Steam-a-Seam2 fusible tape

Threads to match fabrics

Invisible thread

Cardboard or freezer paper

Violet acrylic paint (optional for hand painting the flowers)

Paint brush (optional for hand painting the flowers)

CUTTING

Grape print and light violet: Cut 10 strips each 2" wide x width of fabric.

Light green and two-toned burgundy/green: Cut 4 strips each 3⅞" wide x width of fabric (One option: layer the fabrics right sides together to cut the strips.) Use these strips to cut 40 squares from each fabric 3⅞" x 3⅞".

Tip: There are many ways to make half-square triangle units. How you cut this fabric depends on the method you choose: you can layer fat quarters of each fabric and draw a grid of 3⅞" squares; use Triangles on a Roll paper for paper piecing; or do bias strip piecing. Refer to Harriet Hargrave's The Art of Classic Quiltmaking for all options.

First border: Cut 2 strips 1" x 36½" for the top and bottom borders and 2 strips 1" x 46½" for the side borders.

Second border: Cut 2 strips 4" x 44½" for the top and bottom borders and 2 strips 4" x 46½" for the side borders.

Third border: Cut 2 strips 2" x 47½" for the top and bottom borders and 2 strips 2" x 53½" for the side borders.

Green vines: Cut ⅞"-wide bias strips. Each "S" requires approximately 18"–20"; make 16 strips.

White or light purple for flowers: Using the pattern on page 31, cut 32 circles.

BLOCK ASSEMBLY
Four-Patches

1. Sew a grape-print strip to each light violet strip. Press the seam toward the print fabric.

Sew strips together.

2. Cut the strip set into 2" units.

3. Join the units to make four-patches. They should measure 3½". Make 100 four-patches.

Four-patch unit

Thomas Coyne Winery,
Livermore Valley, California

Half-Square Triangles

1. Draw diagonal lines across the center of the 3⅞" light green squares. Place light green squares right sides together with two-toned burgundy print squares (if you didn't cut them together).

2. Using a ¼" presser foot, sew on each side of the marked diagonal lines.

3. Cut on the drawn line to form the half-square triangle units. Open and press the seams toward the darker fabric. The units should measure 3½". Make 80 half-square triangle units.

QUILT ASSEMBLY

1. Lay out each block as shown. Make 10 A blocks and 10 B blocks.

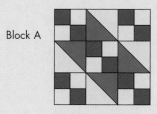

Block A

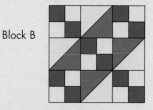

Block B

Road to California Block

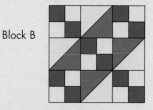

Quilt Assembly Diagram

2. Pin the vertical rows together carefully, matching seams and points of half-square triangles. Stitch, then press the seams in opposite directions from block to block.

3. Sew the vertical rows together following the Quilt Assembly Diagram.

4. Pin the horizontal rows together carefully, matching seams and points of half-square triangles. Sew the horizontal rows together.

BORDERS

Refer to Borders on page 78.

First Border

Sew the top and bottom borders, then the side borders, to the quilt top. Press the seams toward the border.

Second Border

1. Fold each border into quarters and finger-press. Lightly mark the placement for the "S" appliqués onto each quarter of the borders. Refer to the Quilt Assembly Diagram for the orientation of each S.

2. Following the manufacturer's instructions, iron ¼" fusible tape onto the wrong side of each bias strip for the S curves.

3. Pin the S curves onto the quilt top, then fuse to the border following the manufacturer's instructions. With invisible thread in the needle and regular thread in the bobbin, use a narrow zigzag stitch to machine appliqué the S curves to the quilt top.

> **Tip:** *Because it would be difficult to quilt around the flowers, they are added after quilting.*

4. Sew the side borders, then the top and bottom borders, to the quilt top.

Third Border

Sew the side borders, then the top and bottom borders, to the quilt top.

FINISHING

Refer to Quilting Basics on pages 78–79.

1. Press, then trim the corners and edges to square up the quilt top.

2. Layer the backing, batting, and quilt top; baste.

3. Quilt as desired. Small four-petal flowers that mimic the three-dimensional flowers appliquéd later onto the quilt top were stitched in the large green triangle area. Grapes, leaves, and vines were quilted in other areas.

4. Construct and sew the three-dimensional flowers to the quilt.

5. Bind or finish the quilt as desired.

6. Attach a hanging sleeve and label to the back of the quilt.

Making the Three-Dimensional Flowers

1. Using a long basting stitch, stitch ¼" from the edge of each of the white or light purple circles.

2. Using the pattern on page 31, trace and cut out a template for gathering the flowers.

3. Place the template in the center of a stitched circle, and gently pull the gathering stitches until the template is wrapped in a circle shape. Press.

Pull gathering threads to gather circle around template.

4. Remove the template, readjust the stitches, and tie off the threads in back. Clip threads. Press.

5. Thread a needle to match the fabric and tie a knot at the end. Bring the needle up through the center of the gathered circle from the wrong side. Wrap the thread over one edge to the wrong side, and bring the needle back up through the center and pull gently. Repeat. This will form the first flower petals.

Wrap thread around the outside edge from the center and pull to form petals.

Repeat on the opposite edge, then wrap the thread in the same manner around the remaining sides to form the last two petals. To finish, insert the needle into the center and bring the thread back to the wrong side.

Petals formed; bringing thread up to the center

Stitch the loosely gathered edges together in the back and tie off the thread.

6. If you are hand painting the flowers, mist the flowers with water to moisten. Add water to a very small dab of violet paint, then lightly touch the edges of the flower petals so the color "bleeds" into the fabric.

Painting the flowers

You can darken the edges by going back and adding a slightly less watery touch of paint. Experiment on a scrap first.

Finished flowers

7. Let dry and hand-stitch to quilt top at the ends of the S curve.

CURVE OUTLINE

PATTERN FOR GATHERING

PATTERN FOR FLOWERS

Pinot Noir, 62" x 62", Jan Rashid, La Jolla, CA, 1992.

Jan's daughter Laila was working with a winery in Santa Barbara when she encouraged Jan to design a quilt representing one of her favorite wines. A vibrant Pinot Noir was the first inspiration while, in contrast, an elegant Chardonnay inspired a natural sequel. Jan has designed her quilts to reflect both the beauty of the California vineyards and the bounty of their harvest.

California Chardonnay, 73" x 73",
Jan Rashid, La Jolla, CA, 2000.
Photo by Carina Woolrich

Pinot Noir

Finished Quilt Size: 39" x 52"

Machine appliquéd and quilted by Barbara Baker and Jeri Boe, Bend, Oregon.
Photo at top right by Jeri Boe

This fusible appliqué quilt celebrates the Pinot Noir grapes grown in many areas of Oregon. While batiks were used to make this quilt, it would be just as gorgeous created with other fabrics. If you prefer white wine, just reverse the colors and use greens for the grapes and shades of red from red-violet to rust for the leaves. The grapes are made by overlapping small, medium, and large circles, which simplifies the construction of the quilt so it is easy and fun to make, with no small pieces to fuse or stitch down. The surface is embellished with stitching; the amount of embellishment is totally up to you. The quilt could also be hand appliquéd.

GRAPES OF OREGON

If you are a Pinot Noir fanatic, head to Oregon. It is the grape that put Oregon on the international map, and Oregon's cool climate is perfect for growing this grape, and others such as Cabernet Sauvignon, Zinfandel, Pinot Gris, Chardonnay, and Reisling. The Oregon Pinot Noir Club is a great source of information; their website is listed in the directory. Although in general the wineries are spread farther apart than in northern California, you can start in Portland and hit the first wineries of the winery-dense Willamette Valley within half an hour. It's possible to visit ten or more wineries in a single weekend.

FABRIC REQUIREMENTS

Sky blue: 1¼ yards for background

Floral print: ½ yard for bottom background

Medium green: fat quarter for background

Light green: fat quarter or scraps for background

Second medium green: fat quarter or scraps for leaves

Second light green: fat quarter or scraps for leaves

Dark green: fat quarter or scraps for leaves

Assorted purples: fat quarter or scraps for grapes

Teal green: fat quarter or scraps for grape leaves

Medium brown: fat quarter or scraps for vine

Dark brown: fat quarter or scraps for vine

Dark green: ⅜ yard for inner border

Purple: ⅓ yard for middle border and grapes

Outer border and binding: 1¼ yards

Backing: 1½ yards

Batting: 33" x 56"

Threads to match fabrics

Fusible web: 3 yards

Tear-away stabilizer: 3 yards

Threads for decorative stitching: green, purple, and brown rayon

CUTTING

Background: Cut 1 rectangle 29" x 42" (to be trimmed after appliqué is complete).

Borders: Cut 4 strips 2½" wide x width of fabric for the inner border.

Cut 5 strips 1½"-wide x width of fabric for the middle border.

Cut 5 strips 3½" wide x width of fabric for the outer border.

Binding: Cut 6 strips 2½" wide x width of fabric for the binding.

QUILT ASSEMBLY

1. Enlarge the pattern on page 35 465%. Tape the master pattern to a lightbox or large window. Trace all pattern pieces onto the fusible web and cut out the pieces.

2. Fuse the fusible web pieces to the fabrics chosen for each shape. Cut out each design on the line.

3. Arrange floral print on lower section of sky blue background rectangle. Place all pieces onto the background, following the pattern to layer the grapes and leaves. Insert small pieces of coordinating fabric under other pieces to cover any open spaces. Fuse in place according to the manufacturer's instructions.

4. Back the quilt top with tear-away stabilizer or freezer paper. Use your choice of decorative stitches around the raw edges of all the appliqués and satin stitch the leaf veins.

5. After the center panel has been completed, trim it to 27½" x 40½". Be sure to keep the design centered.

BORDERS

Refer to Borders on page 78.

1. Add the side inner borders, then the top and bottom borders. Press the seams toward the center.

2. Add the side middle borders, then the top and bottom borders. Press the seams toward the center.

3. Add the side outer borders, then the top and bottom borders. Press the seams toward the center.

FINISHING

Refer to Quilting Basics on pages 78–79.

1. Press, then trim the corners and edges to square up the quilt top.

2. Layer the quilt top, batting, and backing. Pin, thread, or spray baste.

3. Quilt by machine around the leaves and grapes. Meander quilt in the background and borders. Be careful not to quilt over any satin stitching. Stitch in-the-ditch around the borders.

4. Trim the excess batting and backing and trim the quilt to approximately 39" x 52".

5. Bind or finish as desired.

6. Attach a hanging sleeve and label to the back of the quilt.

Pattern for Pinot Noir is a mirror image of the quilt for fusible appliqué.

Many quilters plan a pilgrimage to the Sisters Outdoor Quilt Show, sponsored by the Stitchin' Post in July. Volunteers hang quilts in every possible nook and cranny. As Don Boyd, wine steward for Sisters commented, "There are more quilts than people." But only until the quilters arrive; then the town is flooded! While you are in town you can do some wine tasting at the Sisters Drug Company. If you love home-made ice cream, try the Marionberry Sundae at the Snow Cap.

If you have the time, head west two and a half hours toward Eugene and stop at three of Don's favorite wineries. The King Estate Winery in the South Willamette Valley boasts a chateau on 880 acres of rolling hills, and offers a picnic area. The WillaKenzie Estate is beautifully situated in a vineyard that has kept part of the acreage in its natural state. Elk Cove Vineyards is an older winery that offers breathtaking views from its hilltop location within an elk preserve.

Emerald Valley

Finished Quilt Size: 48" x 38"

Machine pieced, appliquéd, and quilted by Barbara Baker and Jeri Boe, Bend, Oregon. *Photos taken at Cristom Vineyards, Salem, Oregon by Jeri Boe.*

Strip piecing and fusible appliqué make this a good beginner landscape quilt. Just pay attention to the direction of the stripes. This quilt is fun to make because with just a little extra sewing for the stripes in the fields, the quilter can enjoy spectacular results.

FABRIC REQUIREMENTS

Beige: ⅞ yard for background

Blue: ¼ yard for sky

Medium brown: ½ yard for fields

Green stripe: ½ yard for fields

Medium green: 1 yard for fields and binding

Light, medium, and dark greens: 11 fat quarters in assorted shades for bushes, fields, leaves, mountains, and trees

Scraps: blue, light purple, medium purple, dark purple, tan, brown, and black for the grape clusters and mountains

Light tan: ⅓ yard for the inner border

Dark green: ⅔ yard for the outer border

Backing: 1½ yards

Batting: 42" x 52"

Fusible web: 3 yards

Tear-away stabilizer: 3 yards

Threads to match fabrics

Threads for decorative stitching: purple, green, tan, blue, and brown

CUTTING

Background: Cut one rectangle 38" x 28" (will be trimmed after appliqué is complete)

Fields (medium green): Cut 5 strips 2¼" x 18½" for Field A.

Cut 5 strips 1½" x 16½" for Field B.

Cut 9 strips 2" x 32½" for Field C.

Fields (medium brown): Cut 4 strips 1" x 18½" for Field A.

Cut 5 strips 1" x 16½" for Field B.

Cut 9 strips 1" x 32½" for Field C.

Inner border (light tan): Cut 2 strips 2" x 26½" for side borders and 2 strips 2" x 39½" for top and bottom borders.

Outer border (dark green): Cut 2 strips 5" x 29½" for side borders and 2 strips 5" x 48½" for top and bottom borders.

Backing: Cut one rectangle 42" x 52".

Binding: Cut 5 strips 2½" x width of fabric.

FIELD ASSEMBLY

1. There are three pieced field sections: A, B, and C. Following the cutting instructions, piece together the medium green and medium brown strips in alternating colors. Press the seams in one direction.

Strip Piecing for Field Sections

2. Enlarge the pattern on page 39 555%. Trace the three pieced field patterns onto the fusible web. Fuse to the wrong side of the pieced field fabric, trimming off the excess fabric following the manufacturer's directions.

QUILT ASSEMBLY

1. Trace all other pattern pieces onto the fusible web following the instructions in Quilting Basics on pages 78–79.

2. Layer the individual pieces starting with the sky first, then the mountains, fields, bushes, and trees. Place all shapes on the background and check to make sure there are no gaps or open spaces. If so, fill in with a small piece of fabric. Fuse everything in place.

3. Back the quilt top with tear-away stabilizer. Satin stitch around all the raw edges. Start in the center for the satin stitching and work out toward the borders.

4. Once the satin stitching is done remove the stabilizer and trim the center piece to 36½" x 26½".

5. Referring to Borders on page 78, sew the tan inner side borders, then the top and bottom borders to the quilt top. Press the seams toward the borders.

6. Sew the green outer side borders, then the top and bottom borders to the quilt top. Press the seams toward the borders.

7. Cut a black background piece for each grape cluster. Cut out and place grape pieces on the black backgrounds; fuse grapes in place. Add fusible web to the back of the black background pieces and to the leaves. Position the leaves and grape clusters in the border, and fuse in place. Back the fused area with tear-away stabilizer and satin stitch around the raw edges.

FINISHING

Refer to Quilting Basics on pages 78–79.

1. Press, then trim the corners and edges to square up the quilt top.

2. Layer the quilt top, batting, and backing. Pin or thread baste the layers together.

3. To quilt, stitch in-the-ditch just outside of the satin-stitched shapes. Follow the mountain curves, the lines in the striped fabric, and add circles in the grapes. Quilt grape leaves and tendrils in the green border.

4. Trim the excess batting and backing.

5. Bind or finish as desired.

6. Attach a hanging sleeve and label to the back of the quilt.

Grape Cluster

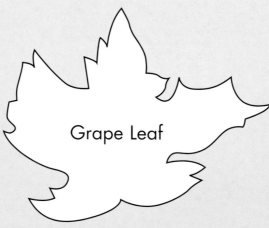

Grape Leaf

Enlarge 200%.

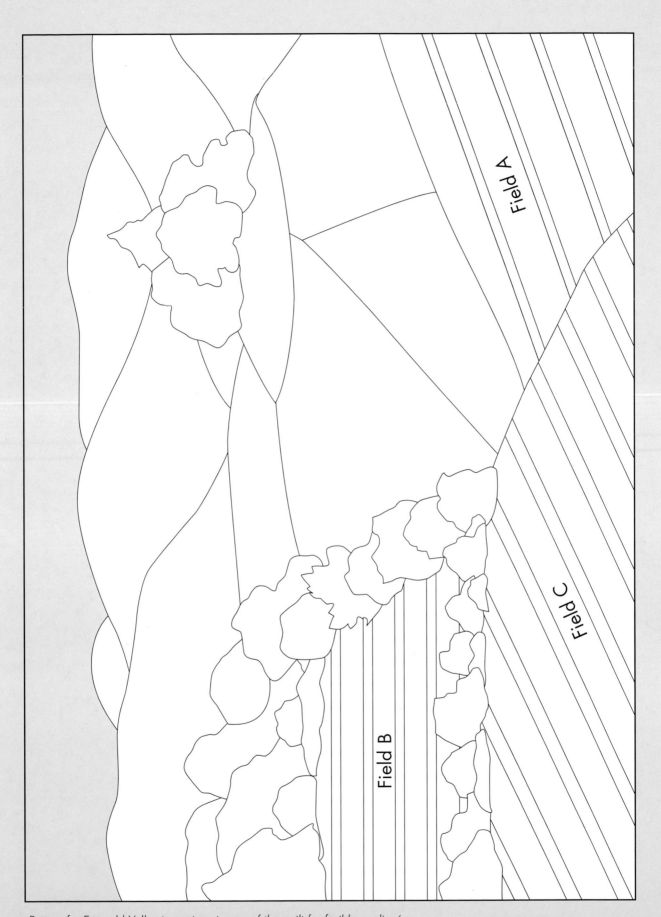

Field A

Field C

Field B

Pattern for Emerald Valley is a mirror image of the quilt for fusible appliqué.

La Vendange, 43" x 26", Kathy Davie, Denver, CO, 1997.

Kathy's husband, Chris, taught her to truly appreciate wines. When a conversation about wine tasting came up, she suddenly saw *La Vendange* in her mind. She wanted to blend the various aspects of winemaking: grapes, vat and bottle storage, the cave, and, of course, tasting, in one seamless art quilt. (And it has the best French bread she's ever stitched.)

The Colors of My Valley, 28" x 28", Anni Donohue, Napa Valley, CA, 2002.

This creation began in early 1992 when Anni decided the time had finally come for her to translate her feelings for her valley. She feels very fortunate to reside in such a colorful environment. This quilt will always have a place in her heart as it represents her home and her return to quilting. She chose the pinwheel block as it is one of her favorites, and used paper-piecing techniques.

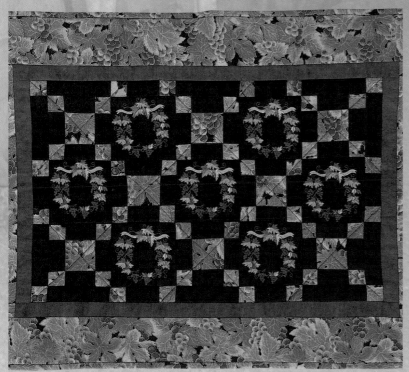

Grapevine Wreath, 28" x 15", Carolyn Bachsmith, Sayville, NY, 2002.

Carolyn not only quilts in the beautiful wine region of North Fork, Long Island, New York; she also owns a quilt store called Patchworks in Sayville, New York. The machine-embroidered grapes are from Pfaff's Martha Pullen card.

Grapes Nouveau

Finished Quilt Size: 65" x 65"

Machine appliquéd and quilted by Barbara Baker and Jeri Boe, Bend, Oregon.
Photo at top left taken at Marsh Red Hills Vineyard by Jeri Boe

Urban Winery

Our glasses are raised to the Wine Goddess, Laurie Lewis, and the Wine Maven, Renée Neely, who decided to open a winery in a slightly offbeat location: an industrial district in downtown Portland. The winery, Hip Chicks Do Wine, is located in an area that is home to several artists, a microbrewery, and the Crystal Springs Rhododendron Gardens. The idea was to offer a spot that people could get to using mass transit or a bike, and, most importantly, that wine should be FUN. From chicks with hips, we say "Thanks for being so creative!"

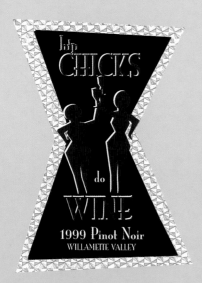

Grapes Nouveau presents a dramatic and graphic way to use the grape-print fabrics you collect on your travels. This striking wallhanging or table topper is made with easy strip piecing and half-square triangles.

FABRIC REQUIREMENTS

Grape print: 1/3 yard for center of blocks

Purple print: 1 1/4 yards for blocks and border (cut lengthwise)

Purple check: 1/3 yard for blocks

Green print: 1/2 yard for blocks

Blue: 1 yard for blocks and border

Green stripe: 3/8 yard for blocks

Black: 4 yards for blocks, border (cut lengthwise), and binding

Backing: 4 yards

Batting: 69" x 69"

Thread: purple, aqua, green and black decorative thread for quilting

CUTTING

Grape print: Cut 1 square 9 1/4" x 9 1/4" for the center block.

Cut 4 squares 6 1/2" x 6 1/2" for the corner blocks.

Purple print: Cut 2 strips 3 3/8" x 11 1/4" and 2 strips 3 3/8" x 17" for the center block. Cut 4 strips 3 1/2" x 41" for the inner border.

Purple check: Cut 8 strips 1 1/2" x 8" and 8 strips 1 1/2" x 10" for the outer corner blocks.

Green print: Cut 4 strips 3" x 12", 4 strips 3" x 14 1/2", and 4 squares 3 3/8" x 3 3/8" for the outer corner block. Cut the 3 3/8" squares in half diagonally.

Blue: Cut 8 strips 4 1/4" x 17" for the strip-pieced block. Cut two squares 9 3/8". Cut each square in half diagonally twice to make 8 triangles for the inner border.

Green stripe: Cut 8 strips 2 1/2" x 17" for the strip-pieced block.

Black:

Cut the following strips for the center block:

2 strips 1 1/2" x 9 1/4"

2 strips 1 1/2" x 11 1/4"

2 strips 1 1/4" x 17"

2 strips 1 1/4" x 18 1/2"

Cut the following strips for the outer corner blocks:

8 strips 1 1/4" x 6 1/2"

8 strips 1 1/4" x 8"

8 strips 1 1/2" x 10"

8 strips 1 1/2" x 12"

4 strips 3" x 12"

4 strips 3" x 14 1/2"

Cut 4 squares 3 3/8" x 3 3/8", then cut in half diagonally.

Cut the following strips for the strip-pieced blocks:

4 strips 3" x 17"

16 strips 1 1/2" x 17"

Cut the following for the inner border:

4 strips 1 1/2" x 41"

8 strips 1 1/2" x 7 1/4"

4 squares 4 1/2" x 4 1/2"

4 squares 5" x 5", then cut the squares in half diagonally.

Cut the following for the outer border:

2 strips 3 1/2" x 59 1/2"

2 strips 3 1/2" x 67 1/2"

Binding: Cut 8 strips 2 1/2" x 40".

BLOCK ASSEMBLY
Center Block

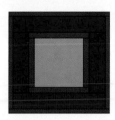

Large Center Block

1. Sew the 1 1/2" x 9 1/4" black strips to the sides of the 9 1/4" grape print square, then sew the 1 1/2" x 11 1/4" strips to the top and bottom. Press the seams toward the center.

2. Sew the 3 3/8" x 11 1/4" purple strips to the sides, then sew the 3 3/8" x 17" strips to the top and bottom. Press the seams toward the center.

3. Sew the 1 1/4" x 17" black strips to the sides, then sew the 1 1/4" x 18 1/2" strips to the top and bottom. Press the seams toward the center.

Outer Corner Blocks

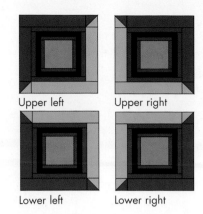

Upper left · Upper right
Lower left · Lower right

Outer Corner Blocks

1. Sew the 1¼" x 6½" black strips to the sides of the 6½" grape print squares, then sew the 1¼" x 8" strips to the top and bottom. Press the seams toward the center.

2. Sew the 1½" x 8" purple check strips to the sides, then the 1½" x 10" purple check strips to the top and bottom of the squares. Press the seams toward the black strips.

3. Sew 1½" x 10" black strips to the sides, then the 1½" x 12" black strips to the top and bottom of the squares. Press the seams toward the purple check strips.

4. Sew one 3" x 12" green strip and one 3" x 12" black strip to opposite sides. Press the seams toward the center.

5. Sew the 3⅜" green triangles to the 3⅜" black triangles to make two half-square triangles for each block. Press the seams toward the black triangles.

6. Sew a green-and-black square to a 3" x 14½" black strip, matching the black sides. Sew a green-and-black square to the 3" x 14½" green strip matching the green sides. Press. Sew these strips to the outer corner blocks following the Assembly Diagram. Press the seams toward the center. Make 4 blocks, noting the orientation of each block.

Strip-Pieced Block

1. Sew a 2½" x 17" green-striped strip to each side of a 3" x 17" black strip. Press the seams toward the black strip.

2. Sew a 1½" x 17" black strip, a 4¼" x 17" blue strip, then a 1½" x 17" black strip to each side of the unit from Step 1. Press the seams toward the center of the block after adding each strip. Repeat to make 4 blocks.

Strip-pieced Block

QUILT TOP ASSEMBLY

1. Sew the blocks together in 3 horizontal rows of 3 blocks each, following the Quilt Assembly Diagram for placement and orientation. Press the seams open.

2. Trim the quilt top to 51½" x 51½".

BORDERS

1. Sew a 1½" x 41" black strip lengthwise to a 3½" x 41" purple strip. Press the seam toward the black strip. Make 4.

2. On the edge of the black strip, mark 4½" from each end as shown. Cut off each strip end at 45° angles as shown.

4½"   4½"

3. Sew a 1½" x 7¼" black strip to each end of the pieced border strip. Gently press the seams toward the black strip. Trim the corners. Make 4.

4. Sew a blue triangle to each end of the pieced border strip. Gently press the seam, without steam, toward the black strip. Make 4.

5. Sew a black triangle to each end. Gently press the seam toward the black triangle.

6. Sew a border unit to the sides of the quilt. Press the seams toward the center.

7. Sew a 4½" black square to each end of top and bottom border units. Press the seams toward the squares. Sew border units to the top and bottom of the quilt. Press the seams toward the center.

8. Sew 3½" x 59½" black outer side borders, then 3½" x 65½" top and bottom borders to the quilt top. Press the seams toward the border.

FINISHING

Refer to Quilting Basics on pages 78–79.

1. Press, then trim the corners and edges to square up the quilt top.

2. Layer the quilt top, batting, and backing. Pin, thread, or spray baste.

3. Quilt as desired.

4. Trim the excess batting and backing.

5. Bind or finish the quilt as desired.

6. Attach a hanging sleeve and label to the back of the quilt.

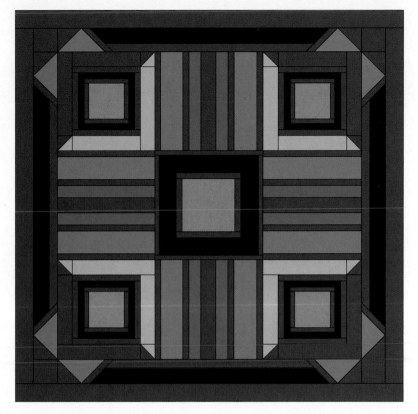

Quilt Assembly Diagram

The grape crush begins.

Whether you like grapes, cherries, or apples, you'll love wandering around Michigan. In the Grand Traverse area you can visit Chateau Grand Traverse, Michigan's oldest winery and guesthouse. Or you can plan a stay at Chateau Chantal, a combination winery, vineyard, and B&B on the Old Mission Peninsula. Leelenau Wine Cellars is the oldest winery on the Leelenau Peninsula, and boasts a spectacular view of Grand Traverse Bay. You can also visit with Tony Ciccone, pop-singer Madonna's father, at Ciccone Vineyards. Another specialty of Michigan's wineries? Ice wine, which requires that the grapes be hand-picked at below-freezing temperatures. Visit Raftshol Vineyard, Arcturos Winery at Black Star Farms, or Chateau Grand Traverse for a bottle of this unusual treat. Best labels in Michigan? Our vote goes to Good Harbor Vineyards.

Colors
of the Vineyard

Finished Quilt Size: 27" x 27"

Stenciled and hand appliquéd by Carol Armstrong, Shingleton, Michigan, with special thanks to Chateau Grand Traverse for their help in understanding the essence of Northern Michigan wines.

The deep blue waters of Lake Michigan, the cherry orchards of the Traverse City area, and the vineyards of northern Michigan provided the inspiration for this wallhanging. A quick stencil technique creates ready-to-appliqué shapes that make this small quilt glow with luminous color.

FABRIC REQUIREMENTS

Unbleached muslin: 1⅜ yards for blocks and labels

Blue: ½ yard for sashing and outer border

Burgundy: ⅓ yard for sashing and binding

Medium Green: ¼ yard for sashing and leaves

Brown, light green, purple, blue: Scraps for appliqués

Backing: 31" x 31"

Batting: 31" x 31"

Green embroidery floss for stems

Threads to match appliqué

Cardstock for stencils

Small Stencil brush

Fabric-ready acrylic paints (available at most hobby and craft stores): blue, red, white, yellow, black, green

Threads to match fabrics

Permanent pens, white and black

Glue stick or Spray adhesive

Optional: acrylic matte varnish and paintbrush, masking tape

CUTTING

Unbleached Muslin:
Cut 4 rectangles 9" x 12½" for the grape blocks (trim to 7" x 10½" after appliqué).

Cut 4 rectangles 5½" x 12½" for the bottle blocks (trim to 3½" x 10½" after appliqué).

Cut 1 strip 5½" x 23" for cherry section (trim to 3½" x 21" after appliqué).

Cut 1 strip 5½" x 26½" for pebble section (trim to 3½" x 24½" after appliqué).

Brown for stems: Cut ⅞"-wide bias strips.

Blue: Cut 2 strips 1" wide for sashing. Cut 4 strips 2" wide for outer border.

Burgundy: Cut 6 strips 1" wide x 10½" for sashing.

Medium green: Cut 1 strip 1" wide for sashing.

Binding: Cut 3 strips 2" wide x width of fabric.

STENCILING

1. Use the patterns on pages 50–51 to trace onto cardstock and cut out each shape to be stenciled.

2. Lay the stencil on the right side of the fabric. Practice painting on scraps to find just the look you want.

Tip: Stencil the bottles onto unbleached muslin. Stencil the other shapes onto fabric that suits each shape, such as green for leaves, red for cherries, and so on. You can also paint each shape on muslin. Refer to the photo of the quilt for color ideas.

Stencil the following appliqué shapes:

Bottles: 1 each of A, B, C, D

Grapes: 4 bunches, 25 grapes per bunch (use the same shape and overlap when appliquéd)

Grape leaf A: 2

Grape leaf B: 2 of each piece

Cherries: 8

Cherry leaves: 2 of each piece C; 3 of each piece D; 3 of each piece E

Pebbles: 10 of each piece A; 13 each of pieces B, C, D

Labels: 4

3. Using the stencil brush and a paint color that is a shade or more darker than your fabric, *lightly* dab paint around the outside edge of the shape. Add just a touch of

lighter color—or less paint—toward the center of the shape. Do not cover all of the fabric with paint unless you are working on muslin. Let dry.

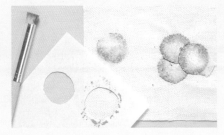

Stenciled grapes

4. Heat-set the paint according to the manufacturer's directions. It is usually sufficient to use a dry iron; be sure to cover the painted shape with paper or a pressing cloth before pressing.

APPLIQUÉ

1. Cut out each stenciled piece approximately ³⁄₁₆" (or just a little over ¼") from the dark edge formed by the paint.

2. Appliqué the shapes, turning under the seam allowance to the painted edge. Stitch the stems on the cherries and grapes first, then follow the order of appliqué for overlapping pieces as noted in the patterns.

3. Use the permanent marking pens to outline the edges of the grapes where they touch, using black pen for the green grapes and white for the purple and blue grapes.

4. Embroider the stems and grape tendrils in green, using a stem stitch.

5. Press the appliqué from the back. Avoid touching the painted fabric directly with the iron; use a press cloth if you need to press from the top.

QUILT ASSEMBLY

1. Trim the blocks to the required size as noted in the cutting directions on page 47.

2. Arrange grape and bottle blocks for top and bottom sections referring to the Quilt Assembly Diagram. Sew 1" x 10 ½" burgundy sashing strips between blocks in each section. Press the seams toward the sashing.

3. Measure through the center of the top and bottom block section from side to side. Cut the 1"-wide blue sashing strip to this measurement; sew between top and bottom sections. Press the seams toward the sashing.

4. Measure through the block section from top to bottom. Cut the 1"-wide blue sashing strip to this measurement; sew to the left side of the quilt. Press the seams toward the sashing.

5. Sew the cherry section to left side of quilt. Press the seams toward the sashing.

6. Measure, trim and sew the 1"-wide medium green sashing strip, then pebble section to the bottom of the quilt. Press the seams toward the sashing.

7. Refer to Borders on page 78 to measure, trim and sew 2"-wide blue borders to the sides, then to the top and bottom of the quilt. Press seams toward the borders.

FINISHING

Refer to Quilting Basics on pages 78–79.

1. Press, then trim the corners and edges to square up the quilt top.

2. Layer the quilt top, batting, and backing. Pin or thread baste the layers together. Avoid stitching through the painted fabrics.

3. Quilt around each motif and along the edges of all the blocks. Add some wandering lines in and around the pebble section. Fill the cherry section with parallel curved lines 1" apart and quilt the grape blocks with straight diagonal lines also 1" apart.

4. Trim the excess batting and backing.

5. Bind or finish as desired.

6. Attach a hanging sleeve and label to the back of the quilt.

Wine Labels

1. Create your own labels from muslin or other fabric, or copy the pattern on page 51. Use a black Pigma pen for the lettering and outlining the grapes and leaf. Using a small brush, stencil the corner triangles and paint the grape and leaf. Use masking tape or cut a stencil to define the outside edge of the label.

2. Cut out and use a glue stick or adhesive spray (spray outside) the labels in place now, OR add a special optional touch with acrylic varnish: Lightly coat each label front and back with matte acrylic varnish.

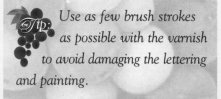
Tip: Use as few brush strokes as possible with the varnish to avoid damaging the lettering and painting.

After the varnish is thoroughly dry paint the back of the label with white paint.

Quilt Assembly Diagram

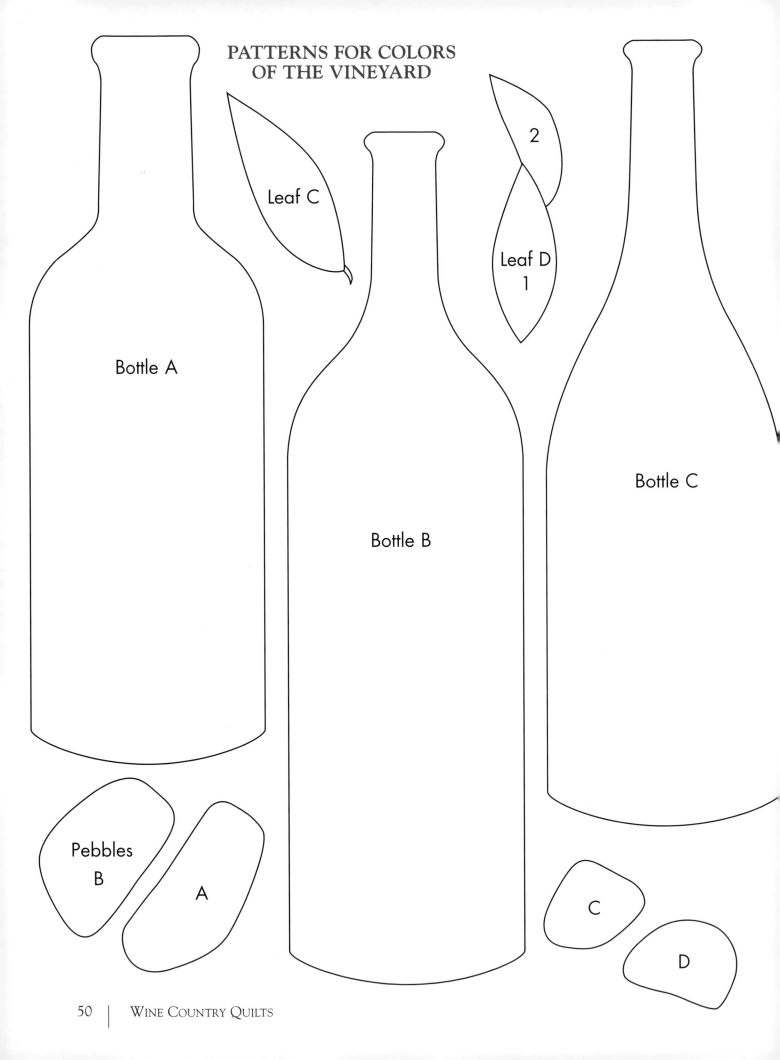

PATTERNS FOR COLORS OF THE VINEYARD

Leaf C

Leaf D
1

2

Bottle A

Bottle B

Bottle C

Pebbles
B

A

C

D

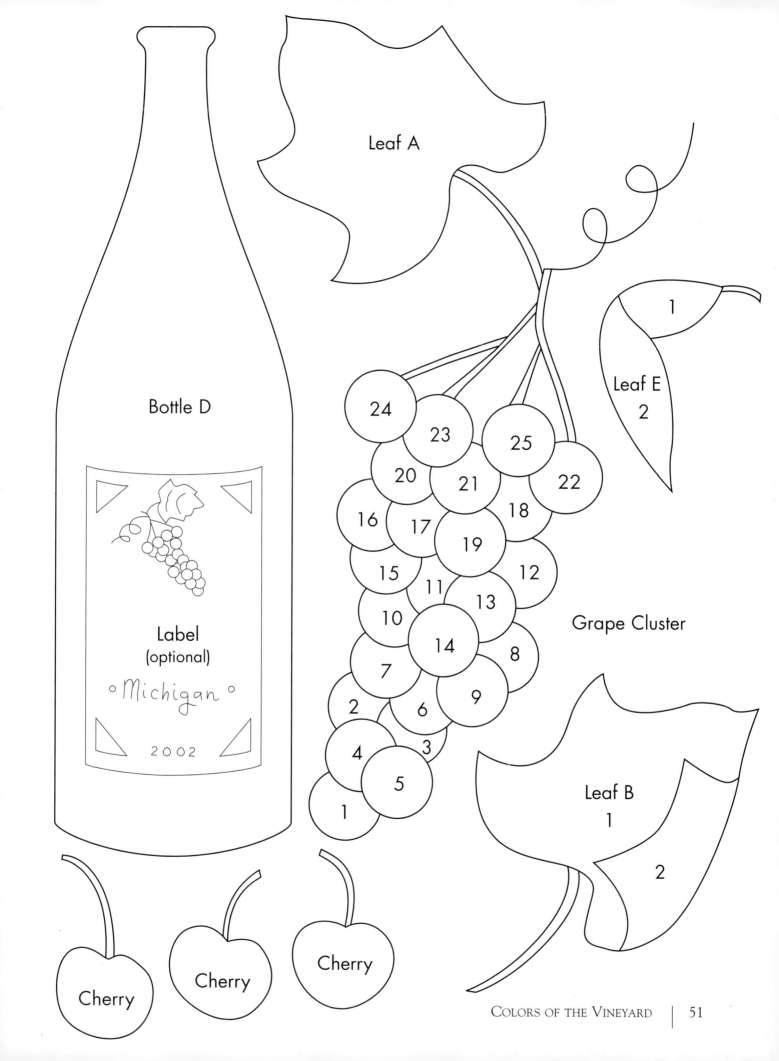

Leaf A

Bottle D

Leaf E
1
2

Label
(optional)

Michigan

2002

Grape Cluster

Leaf B
1

2

Cherry

Cherry

Cherry

In the Arbor

Wine prepares the heart for love—unless you take too much. Ovid

By making this wine vine known to the public, I have rendered my country as great a service as if I had enabled it to pay back the national debt.

Thomas Jefferson

At least a part of the evolution of wine is owed to the fact that it was considered safer to drink than milk, juice, and water, which could spoil easily. Louis Pasteur stated, "Wine can be considered with good reason as the most healthful and most hygienic of all beverages."

Finished Size: 44" x 49½"

Designed, pieced, appliquéd, embroidered, and quilted by Phyllis Norton Hoffman, Birmingham, Alabama

A trellis covered with vines, leaves, and grapes runs through this quilt, evoking the lushness of a vineyard. Perle cotton tendrils hang from the clusters in delicate curls. Create a cozy corner in your home where you can sit and reminisce about days spent touring the vineyards or putting up grape jelly in your country kitchen.

FABRIC REQUIREMENTS

Lavender sky print: ½ yard for background

White print: ½ yard for background

Cream print: ½ yard for background

Tan print: ¾ yard for lattice

Brown print: ¾ yard for lattice

Green/purple print: 1¼ yards (includes binding) for lattice background

Brick print: ¼ yard

Green print: 1 yard for vines

Assorted green prints and solids: 1½ yards total for leaves

Assorted purple and pink prints: ¾ yard total for grapes

Backing: 3 yards

Batting: 49" x 54"

Thread to match fabrics

Quilting thread

Invisible thread

Green perle cotton

Cardboard

Spray starch

Bias Bars, ¼" and ½" (optional)

CUTTING

Lavender sky print: Cut 3 strips 4¼" x width of fabric, then cut into 24 squares. Cut the squares in half diagonally twice to make quarter-square triangles.

White/mint print: Cut 6 strips 2¼" x width of fabric. Cut these strips into 12 strips 2¼" x 8½", and 24 rectangles 2¼" x 3¾".

Cream/green print: Cut 6 strips 2¼" x width of fabric. Cut these strips into 12 strips 2¼" x 8½", and 24 rectangles 2¼" x 3¾".

Tan print: Cut 11 strips 2¼" x width of fabric. Cut these strips into 22 strips 2¼" x 8½", and 44 rectangles 2¼" x 3¾".

Brown print: Cut 11 strips 2¼" x width of fabric. Cut these strips into 22 strips 2¼" x 8½", and 44 rectangles 2¼" x 3¾".

Green/purple print: Cut 5 strips 4¼" x width of fabric. Cut 44 squares 4¼" x 4¼", then cut squares in half diagonally twice to make quarter-square triangles.

Brick print: Cut 1 strip 6" x 22½".

Vines (green print): Cut enough 1"-wide bias strips to make 190".

Cut enough 1½"-wide bias strips to make 315".

Leaves (assorted greens): Cut the following using the patterns on pages 55–56.

14 each A and AR (A reversed)

4 each B and BR (B reversed)

6 each C and CR (C reversed)

8 each D and DR (D reversed)

Grapes (assorted purple and pink prints): Cut 124 grapes using pattern E on page 56.

BLOCK ASSEMBLY

1. Sew 2 lavender sky triangles to a 2¼" x 3¾" cream rectangle. Press the seams toward the rectangle. Make 24. Repeat to make 24 pieced units using lavender sky triangles and white 2¼" x 3¾" rectangles. Press.

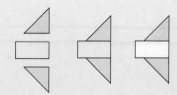

Make 24 of each.

2. Make 44 pieced units as you did in Step 1 using the green/purple print triangles and tan 2¼" x 3¾" rectangles. Make 44 pieced units using the green/purple print triangles and the brown 2¼" x 3¾" rectangles.

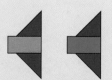

Make 44 of each.

3. Sew the pieced units from Steps 1 and 2 to 2¼" x 8½" strips as shown below to make the number of units indicated. Trim each block to 6" square to make the Lattice Blocks. Press.

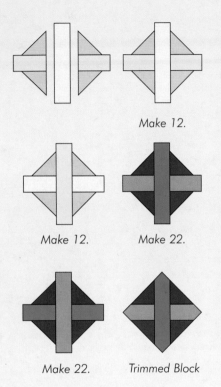

Make 12.

Make 12.   Make 22.

Make 22.   Trimmed Block

QUILT ASSEMBLY

1. Follow the Assembly Diagram to sew the blocks together into 8 horizontal rows of 8 blocks. Press the seams in opposite directions from row to row.

2. Sew 2 sets of 2 blocks together; add to each short end of the brick print strip to make the bottom row. Press the seams toward the center.

3. Sew the rows together. Press the seams in alternate directions.

APPLIQUÉ

1. Sew the 1"-wide green print bias strips end-to-end to make the vines, then sew the 1½"-wide bias strips together. Fold the strips in half lengthwise with wrong sides together. Stitch ¼" from the cut edge. Trim the seam allowance to ⅛". Press the bias tube flat, centering the seam on the back so the raw edge is not visible from the front.

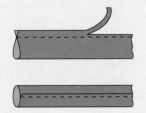

Trim the seam to ⅛", press with seam centered on back.

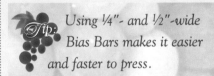

Tip: Using ¼"- and ½"-wide Bias Bars makes it easier and faster to press.

2. To make the leaves, place each leaf A with leaf Ar right sides together. Stitch ¼" from the outer edge, leaving a small opening to turn the leaves. Clip the curves and turn right side out; whipstitch the openings closed.

3. Prepare the remaining leaves using patterns B and Br, C and Cr, and D and Dr.

4. To make the grapes, cut a circle of cardboard the finished size of the grape. Sew a gathering stitch about ⅛" from the outer edge of each grape. Place the cardboard circle on the wrong side of the

fabric and pull the gathering stitches to enclose the circle. Spray lightly with starch and press. Cool, then slightly loosen the gathering stitch to remove the cardboard circle. Make 124 grapes.

Sew a gathering stitch   Gathered grape
⅛" from the edge.

5. Referring to the photograph, randomly position the bias strips and machine- or hand-appliqué in place. The vines on this quilt were machine appliquéd using invisible thread and a blind stitch.

6. Position the leaves and grape clusters and appliqué to the quilt top.

7. With green perle cotton, embroider tendrils using a stem stitch.

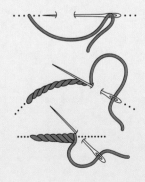

Stem stitches

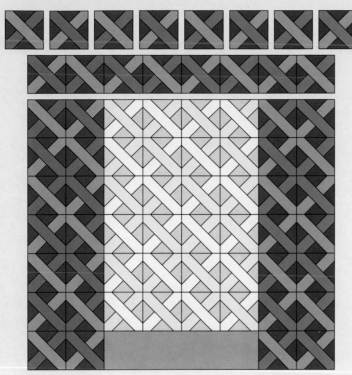

Quilt Assembly Diagram

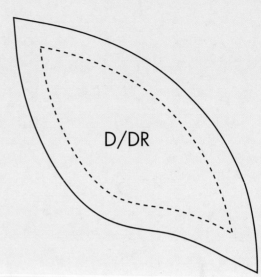

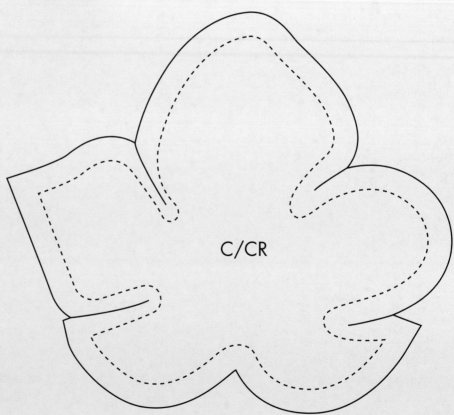

FINISHING

Refer to Quilting Basics on pages 78–79.

1. Press, then trim the corners and edges to square up the quilt top.

2. Layer the quilt top, batting, and backing. Pin, thread, or spray baste.

3. Quilt as desired.

4. Trim the excess batting and backing.

5. Bind the quilt with the leftover green/purple fabric or finish as desired.

6. Attach a hanging sleeve and label to the back of the quilt

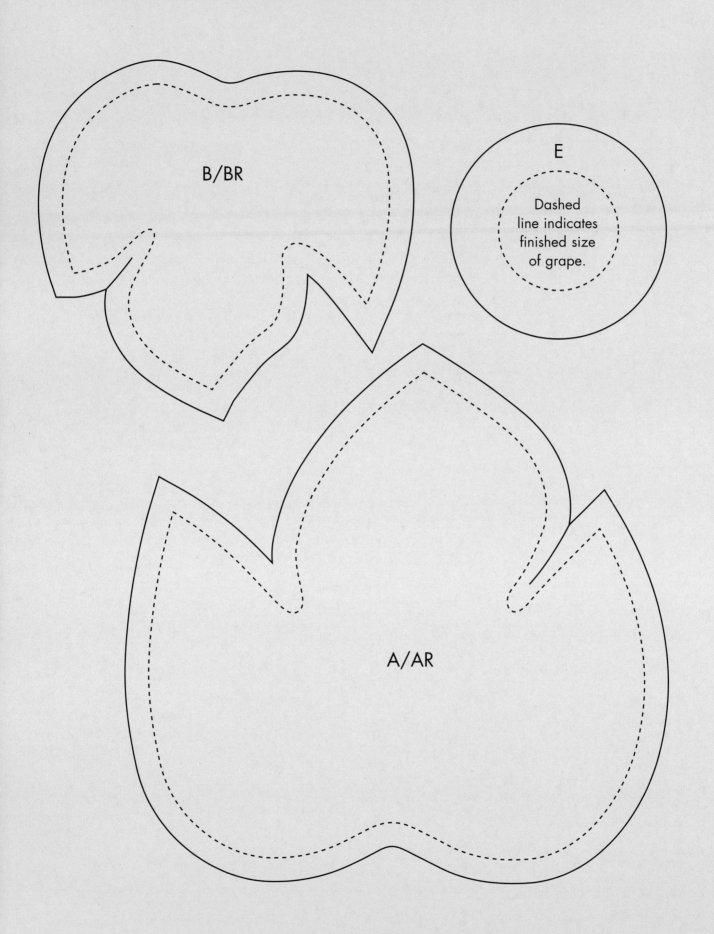

B/BR

E

Dashed line indicates finished size of grape.

A/AR

In Vino Veritas, 21½" x 40½", 2002.

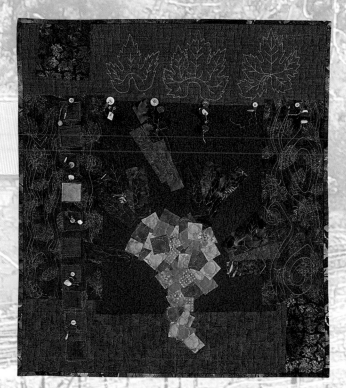

Grapes V, 31" x 36", Babette Grunwald, Prosser, WA, 2002.

Grapes IV, 21½" x 40½", 2002.

Babette Grunwald uses a collage technique, making her quilts look like abstract paintings. The scraps of fabric are the brush strokes a painter might use and the free-motion quilting defines the design lines. After moving to Prosser, heart of Washington's wine country, she was inspired by her environment to start two new series: one illustrates the contrast and tension between the irrigated agriculture and the native ecosystem of eastern Washington, the other depicts grapes and her love for viticulture.

Grapes I, 24" x 17½", Babette Grunwald, Prosser, WA, 2001.

October, 26" x 19", Sondra Townsend Donabed, Newton, MA, 1999.
Photo by David Caras, courtesy of Quilter's Newsletter Magazine

Sondra had been working with monoprints on a glorious autumn day and picked up some large grape leaves to experiment with on her way back into the studio. The rest of the day was spent printing leaves, negative leaves, and ghost leaves on silk charmeuse which eventually developed into an ongoing mini-series representing the months.

Private Collection

Finished Quilt Size: 20" x 20"

Finished block size: 4"

Designed, machine pieced, appliquéd, and quilted by Jan Smiley,
Fort Mill, South Carolina

If you know anyone with an extensive wine collection, this quilt would make a great gift. You can add to the number of bottles on the rack to reflect a larger collection.

A warm welcome awaits you at
Livermore Valley Cellars, California

WINERIES AND THE ARTS

Many wineries and organizations are passionately committed to the arts and architecture. The list includes, but is not limited to, the following:

Copia: The American Center for Wine, Food and the Arts in downtown Napa; a good place to begin or end a journey in Napa.

Clos Pegase, where owner Jan Shrem has made his private art collection available for public viewing in Napa.

Heller Estate/Durney Vineyards, Carmel Valley

Hess Collection Winery, Napa, with its modern art collection housed in a beautiful gallery.

Messina Hof, in Bryan, Texas, hosts an art competition each year and uses the winning images as labels for future vintages.

Mumm of Napa Valley has a constantly changing exhibit of photographs.

DiRosa Preserve in Sonoma features an art collection both indoors in a restored home and outdoors in a glorious natural setting.

Channing Daughters on North Fork, Long Island, New York, features wood sculptures by Walter Channing.

Kenwood Vineyards of Sonoma has been featuring the works of major artists on their labels series for over twenty-five years.

Chateau St. Michelle, Woodinville, Washington has dedicated a series of labels to works by glass artists such as Dale Chihuly.

Duckhorn Vineyard, St. Helena, California, who commission paintings of a pair of ducks on their labels.

FABRIC REQUIREMENTS

Greens: several shades of scraps totaling ⅝ yard for block backgrounds

Reds: several shades of scraps in medium and dark values totaling ⅓ yard for wine bottles

Wood grain: ⅓ yard for wine rack sashing and intersections

Backing: 24" square

Batting: 24" square

Binding: ¼ yard

Fusible web: ¾ yard

Coordinating threads for piecing and machine quilting

Optional: Adhesive spray or glue

CUTTING

Block backgrounds: Cut 13 squares 4½" x 4½".

Cut 2 squares 9" x 9"; cut in half diagonally twice to make 8 setting triangles for the quilt sides.

Cut 2 squares 4⅞" x 4⅞"; cut in half diagonally to make 4 triangles for the quilt corners.

Wine bottles: From medium reds, freehand cut 13 asymmetric circles approximately 4½" in diameter. If you prefer, you can make a circle template using the bottom of a wine bottle, a coffee mug, plastic container, or a small saucer.

From darker reds, freehand cut 13 smaller asymmetric circles, ranging in diameter from 1½" to 2½".

Wood-grain fabric:

Cut 2 strips 1¼" wide, then cut 2 strips 1¼" x 25" and 2 strips 1¼" x 15½" for wine rack sashing strips.

Cut 3 strips 1¼" wide, then cut 18 pieces 1¼" x 4½" and 2 pieces 1¼" x 6" for wine-bottle-rack sashing strips.

Cut 1 strip 1⅜" wide, then cut 24 squares 1⅜" x 1⅜" for the intersecting squares of the lattice strips.

Backing and batting: Cut a 24" square of each.

Binding: Cut 3 strips 2¼" wide x width of fabric.

BLOCK ASSEMBLY

Wine bottle bottoms

1. Arrange and appliqué the smaller red circles on top of the larger red circles using your choice of fusible web, adhesive spray, glue, or machine appliqué.

2. Arrange and appliqué the layered red circles on the green squares. Remember the blocks will be on point to resemble the bottom of bottles in a wine rack, so the circles should be placed close to the seam allowances on the bottom two corners of each block.

Summertime at Bedell Cellars, Long Island, New York

QUILT ASSEMBLY

1. Arrange the green appliquéd blocks and the green setting triangles in a layout that pleases you. Note that the blocks are set on point.

2. Referring to the Quilt Assembly Diagram, sew the 4½" wood-grain lattice strips, blocks, and side and corner triangles to form diagonal rows. Press the seams toward the lattice strips.

3. Sew the rows together, alternating with 1¼" x 6", 1¼" x 15½", and 1¼" x 25" sashing strips to complete the top.

4. Appliqué the 24 wood-grain squares at each of the lattice-strip intersections, using your preferred method.

FINISHING

Refer to Quilting Basics on pages 78–79.

1. Press, then trim the corners and edges to square up the quilt top.

Note: When you square up the quilt, you will also be trimming away some corners of the appliquéd wood-grain fabric squares.

2. Layer the quilt top, batting and backing. Pin baste, thread baste, or use spray basting material.

3. Quilt by hand or machine as desired.

4. Trim the excess batting and backing. Square up the quilt.

5. Bind or finish the quilt as desired.

6. Attach a hanging sleeve and label to the back of the quilt.

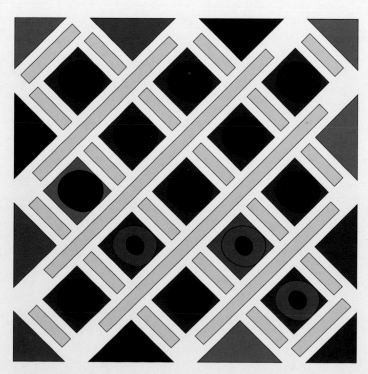

Quilt Assembly Diagram

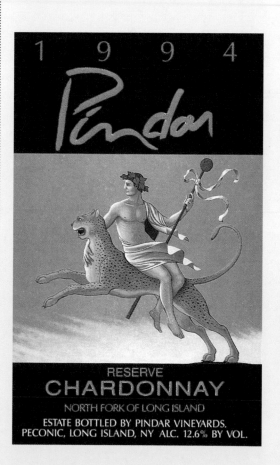

Martha's Vin Rosé, 84" x 90", Mary Lou Fahrni, Lakewood, CO, 1996. *Photo by Melissa Karlin Mahoney, courtesy of Quilter's Newsletter Magazine*

Inspiration can come from a variety of sources: Martha found a Mountain Mist pattern called "Martha's Vineyard" at a garage sale in Missouri, and wanted to use the shaded pink fabric that is featured in her quilt.

Baltimore Album Wedding Quilt, 36" x 28", Donna Hall, Napa Valley, CA, 1997.

Donna designed this wallhanging in the traditional Baltimore Bride style for her daughter, who was married in Baltimore in 1977. It includes the state flower and bird of Maryland—the Black-eyed Susan and the Baltimore Oriole—for her husband, Robert A. Dunn, and the California Poppy and quail for Donna's daughter Patty Hall. The three blue eggs in the nest signify the three daughters born to their union. The three varieties of grapes represent their life in the Napa Valley, and Robert's long-time involvement in the wine industry for Beaulieu Vineyard and Sutter Home Winery.

Forest Star, Linda Glantz, 90" x 108", Holley, NY, 1999.

Linda's glorious quilt was inspired by a trip through the wine country of Naples, New York.
It won Viewer's Choice at the Country Neighbor's Quilt Guild show.

Wine Tasting *with Friends*

WHAT DO YOU TASTE?

This is *the* question to ask any time you taste wine. The pros have made this an art form. It is fun to start a list at your party of the descriptive words your guests come up with. What the heck, award prizes for the most original descriptions; this can be as simple as a pack of funny cocktail napkins, or one of the wine bags you made following the directions on page 69. It's amazing to read what the professional oenophiles (wine lovers) come up with. To get you started, a very informal poll conducted with other tasters met along the wine trail yielded these possibilities: barbecue in a bottle (meaning smoky); pretty; snappy; uplifting; heady; big; grapefruity; grassy; earthy; full-bodied; a full bouquet of flowers; fresh-cut grass; sweaty armpits (!). Make small blank books or forms to be used to evaluate the appearance, aroma, and overall impression of each wine tasted.

Choose a theme, invite at least six friends, clean a lot of wine glasses (or ask your buddies to bring some of their own), dig out your cork-screws, and get ready to pour. That's really all it takes to host a wine tasting party. When you do plan a tasting during the holidays or as a special fund-raising event, it can't hurt to do it in style with the *Puttin' on the Glitz Table Topper*, Wine Charms, and *Blind Wine-Tasting Bags* on pages 67–68. Just a touch of easy elegance with simple materials, and some great wines, and you've got the makings for a wonderful evening.

Tip: One suggestion to get the evening rolling is to offer supplies for making your own wine glass charms to identify each person's glass. All it takes are some rings used for earrings (available at most craft or bead stores), a variety of beads, some charms, and anything else you can think of. Everyone goes home with his or her own personalized wine charm.

As far as the theme goes, there are a few ways to go. You can supply all the wines ($ cha-ching), or (more fun for everyone) get everyone involved and ask each participant to bring a bottle. The focus can be a particular vintage (1997 was a very good year) of the same red varietal, such as Merlot or Zinfandel, or a white: Chardonnay, Sauvignon Blanc, or Viognier. If you really feel like putting on the glitz around the holidays, ask everyone to bring a bottle of sparkling wine. Just be sure to establish a tight price range.

When creating the invitations, ask that your guests *not* wear any perfumes or after-shaves: these can throw off the nose or "bouquet" of the wine.

What about food to accompany the tastings? Simple crackers will do; lots of wineries offer oyster crackers or other plain crackers. The idea is that you don't want the flavors of the food to interfere with the taste of the wines.

Dinner can be potluck; just be sure to ask your guests to bring something specific such as a salad or side dish so you don't have too much of one good thing. Recipes follow for some après tasting treats.

When you pour from each bottle, plan on two ounces or less per glass. The type of glass isn't crucial, but you might ask the participants to bring some along so you have enough. The glasses should be large enough for the wine to swirl around in, but keep the amount of wine poured low, or you'll lose control of the tasting party quickly. Providing paper cups for spitting is an appropriate thing to do. Professionals *do* spit; that's how they are able to taste more than two wines a day.

WHAT TO LOOK FOR, SMELL, AND TASTE

For the more serious tasters among the crowd, a white surface or poster board to hold the glass up to is recommended for checking the color. First of all, the wine should

Wine Tasting Here

Made by Deb Caulo of Village Floorcloths, Norwich, Vermont
This beautiful invitation was originally made as a floorcloth, but it works just as well as a welcome sign for your wine tasting.

look clear and brilliant. On to color: usually (but not always) younger reds tend toward purple hues, older reds toward a rustier red; young whites tend to be lighter in color, older whites will take on a more golden yellow hue. Then there are the legs; those squiggly little lines of color that slowly (or quickly) run down the side of the glass that indicate the alcohol level.

For sparkling wines, the bubbles should be the size of a pinpoint as well as persistent.

Ever wonder why you are offered a small taste of the wine you just ordered when you are dining out? It is not meant to humiliate you. If it's bad, you'll smell a musty, wet cardboard aroma. Send it back confidently with a smile.

Ready, Set: Swirl, Sniff, Sip, and Savor!

One not only drinks wine, one smells it, observes it, tastes it, sips it, and one talks about it.
King Edward VII

Swirling: Hold the glass by the base, and give it a swirl. This releases all those wonderful aromas. It's easiest to swirl a glass with its base flat on a table. Be gentle; you don't want to shower your neighbor. Are there legs? Fortified sweet wines tend to be leggy.

Sniffing: Tip the glass up, stick your nose down into it, and take a good, hearty sniff. This is the "nose" the pros refer to, and it will be different for everyone. Take your time and record what you smell. What you smell is what you get. Blackberry? Wood? Leather? Currant? Yum!

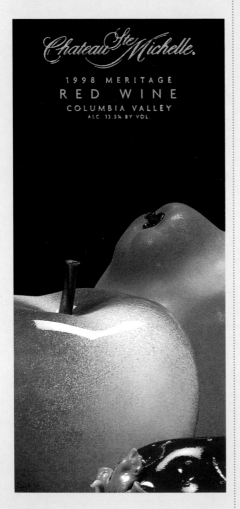

Photo by Ted Bennett, Navarro Vineyards

Sipping: Take a small sip. Don't gargle, but definitely swirl it around in your mouth. The second part of tasting is to draw some air into your mouth while you hold the wine in your mouth (a difficult thing to perfect). Focus. Think about what you are tasting as well as how the wine feels in your mouth. Is it round and rich, or thin and angular? Then either spit (recommended if you will be tasting a *lot* of wine) or swallow.

Finish: This is the official term for the aftertaste. If there is a pleasant, lingering taste in your mouth, that's another good thing. If it is a young red wine, tannins—which tend to make your mouth pucker a bit—are necessary for a red wine's ability to age.

Pace yourself, and drink a lot of water between tastes. Eating a plain cracker before you try the next wine is also a good "palate-cleansing" idea.

As you taste each wine, note your overall impression: Is the wine's appearance, aroma, flavor, and finish seamless or disjointed? How does it compare to the other wines in the group? Most important, did it tempt you back for another sip? Use a simple numbering system—one being the best overall and five being the lowest rating—to keep track of your impressions. The host can tally the scores, then reveal which wine received the highest overall rating. Return the scoring sheets to your guests, then encourage them to note the vintage, producer, and price on their sheets.

Some projects follow for making your wine tasting party a memorable event. Invite a friend to help! This is the pre-party sewing party. They are simple projects that beginning sewers can tackle with confidence.

Puttin' on the *Glitz* Table Topper

Finished Size: 54" x 71"

Designed by Cyndy Lyle Rymer and Jennifer Rounds. Photographed at Merryvale Vineyards

We just couldn't help ourselves when we went fabric shopping. The large rolls of tulle and silks called to us. The construction of the table topper pictured above was kept simple.

FABRIC REQUIREMENTS

Iridescent gold organza: 4 yards

Silk dupioni in greens, purples, maroon, and dark gold: ⅛- to ¼-yard each

Freezer paper

Glue stick

Threads to match fabrics

¼" fusible adhesive tape (optional)

ASSEMBLY

1. Fold a long length of iridescent gold organza in half crosswise. Fold the edges under ¼", then fold another ¼" to create a hem. Stitch the edges together with a simple decorative stitch. Nonsewers could use a fusible adhesive tape to seal the edges.

MERRYVALE

1999

CABERNET SAUVIGNON

NAPA VALLEY

2. Enlarge the leaf patterns 200%, and trace onto the shiny side of freezer paper.

3. Iron freezer paper templates to the wrong side of the silk dupioni fabrics. Cut grape leaves and grapes in a variety of shapes and sizes. Invite a friend to help, and find a spot where you can spread out the length of the tablecloth.

4. Position all of the leaves on the right side of the folded length of fabric, then check for color balance. (Leave the middle free of leaves for the bottles and bowls of crackers.) When you like what you see, pin all of the leaves in place.

5. Lightly glue the leaves and grapes in place.

6. The grapes and leaves on the table topper were sewn with the feed dogs down and free-motion stitching. You can also use a regular stitch with the feed dogs engaged.

7. Tack some hanging beads on the corners, and you've got a special staging area for the tasting.

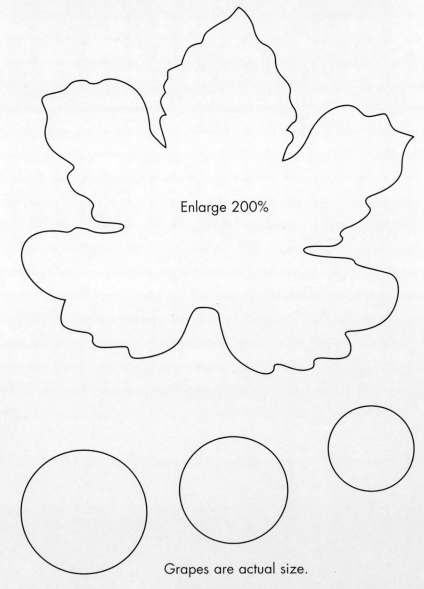

Enlarge 200%

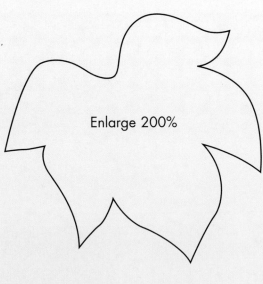

Enlarge 200%

Grapes are actual size.

Blind Wine-Tasting Bags

Designed by Cyndy Lyle Rymer and Jennifer Rounds.

Part of the fun of a tasting party is to have no idea what you are tasting; your guests will know the varietal (such as Chardonnay or Zinfandel) you are trying, but they won't know the winery each came from. These bags are not only a perfect way to hide the labels, they are easy to make.

FABRIC REQUIREMENTS

Silk, organza, or other fabric:
One piece approximately 6" x 38" (see note below)

Strip of contrasting fabric

Ribbon or covered cording

Note: If the fabric is transparent, you might want to double the layer of fabric; this requires twice the length.

ASSEMBLY

1. Optional: Use a grape leaf to hide the label: Before you sew the side seams for the bag, machine appliqué the smaller of the grape leaf shapes (page 68) from the table topper onto the middle of the bag.

2. Fold the fabric in half lengthwise. Use a wide zigzag stitch to seam the two sides. Turn the bag right side out.

3. To create the casing for the closure, cut a strip of contrasting fabric 2" x 12". Create a hem on either end by turning the edge under ¼" twice. Fold both lengthwise edges in toward the center and press.

4. Fold the top of the bag to the inside so there is a 5½" overlap.

5. Position the casing strip on the bag 5" from the top. Topstitch the top and bottom of the strip, leaving the ends open to insert the ribbon or cording. Put a safety pin on the leading end of the ribbon or cording, and use the pin to guide the cord through the casing.

Insert the wine bottle, close the bag, and tie.

Post Wine-Tasting Dinner

Why not extend the wine tasting party for a few hours and enjoy a good meal together? Here are some ideas to help with the menu planning, courtesy of Tricia O'Brien, a professional caterer and cooking teacher in Oakland, California. Make it a potluck dinner, and the "work" of the party won't take over your life!

1 tsp. chopped jalapeño pepper

1 Tbsp. chopped cilantro

2 Tbsp. ginger

1 Tbsp. garlic

1 cup small shrimp, coarsely chopped

2 cups chicken apple sausage

1 Tbsp. peanut oil

20–30 round wonton wrappers

1 small bowl of water

CHINESE PESTO INGREDIENTS

2 bunches of cilantro (use food processor to chop)

2 cloves garlic

2 tsp. fresh ginger root

1 tsp. orange peel

8 basil leaves

1 green onion

1 Tbsp. light soy sauce

2 Tbsp. dry sherry

2 Tbsp. white vinegar

2 Tbsp. sesame oil

2 tsp. Hoisin sauce (or sweet chili sauce)

2 tsp. granulated sugar

½ tsp. Chinese chili sauce

DRAGON DUMPLINGS WITH SHRIMP

Makes 30 dumplings

These delicious little bundles make wonderful hors d'oeuvres to serve during a white wine tasting, or as an appetizer before serving the Chicken with Red Wine and Fruit that follows. You'll get the hang of folding and sealing the dumplings after you make a few. Invite a friend to help. Be sure not to overfill—the dumplings will tear or fall apart. If you aren't sure where to find wonton wrappers, try the vegetable/fruit section of your supermarket.

1. In a medium skillet, sauté the jalapeño pepper, cilantro, ginger, and garlic in peanut oil for a few minutes, being careful not to burn the garlic.

2. In a medium bowl, mix together the jalapeño pepper mix with the shrimp and sausage.

3. To make the dumplings, hold a wonton wrapper in the palm of your hand. Scoop a little less than one teaspoon of the filling onto the center of the wrapper; too much filling will tear the wonton.

4. Using the fingers of both hands, gently gather the rounded edges together and dip your index finger into the water bowl and run along the edge of the wrapper so the sides will stick together. It should look like a half-moon shape. With the flat side up, tap the middle down and draw the two pointed sides together so they meet. Again dip your index finger into the water to attach the two points together, slightly overlapping them. Make sure that all sides are closed.

5. Repeat until all of the filling, or the wrappers, are gone. These can now be laid out on a cookie sheet and frozen; they will keep for up to a month.

6. Bring water or stock to boil in a large stockpot. When boiling, add dumplings and cook until they float to the top and the ingredients inside are cooked, about 4–5 minutes. These are also excellent left in a half-moon shape and cooked like a pot sticker.

Serve with toothpicks, and Chinese Pesto drizzled over the top.

CHINESE PESTO

Makes 1½ cups

This is a wonderful pesto sauce made from cilantro. It can be used over vermicelli or udon noodles, but is best over Dragon Dumplings.

Place the cilantro, garlic, ginger, orange peel, basil, and green onion in a food processor. Blend for one minute, then add the remaining ingredients. Pour into a blender and puree the mixture about twenty seconds and transfer to a small bowl. This may be made up to one day in advance. It may discolor due to the cilantro, but will perk up with a little lemon juice.

CHICKEN WITH RED WINE AND FRUIT

Serves 6

This is reminiscent of a traditional European stew. The combination of the dried fruit steeped with the red wine, and the fresh herbs and onions, makes it delicious by itself or served with rice or mashed potatoes. Your house will smell delicious as this simmers away on top of the stove.

1. Combine the fruit and the red wine in a medium saucepan and bring to a slow boil. Turn down to simmer for 15–20 minutes. Remove from heat and set aside.

2. In a sauté pan, heat the olive oil and add the diced onions and whole garlic. Sauté for 8–10 minutes or until the onions are translucent. Add the sugar and stir. Remove from heat and set aside.

3. Using a large saucepan, add the butter and salt and pepper and brown the chicken over medium-high heat for about 10 minutes or so, turning the pieces as they need it. Brown on both sides. Add the sautéed onions, garlic, one cup of the fruit/wine liquid, the chicken stock, thyme, sage, and bay leaf. Add flour to the reserved ½ cup of the fruit/wine liquid to thicken; add to ingredients in the pan. Allow flavors to meld by simmering for about 25–35 minutes. Serve on a platter with a sprinkle of parsley as garnish.

1 lb. dried figs, cherries, prunes (pitted), apricots or other dried fruit, left whole or cut in half

3 cups full-bodied red wine

3 Tbsp. olive oil

1 whole onion, diced

4 garlic cloves, left whole

½ tsp. sugar

6 Tbsp. butter

salt and pepper to taste

1 whole chicken, cut into eight pieces

3 cups chicken stock

2 Tbsp. each fresh thyme and sage

1 large bay leaf

2 Tbsp. flour

2 Tbsp. fresh Italian parsley, finely chopped for garnish

SIMPLEST WINE COUNTRY DESSERT

Marinate some fruit in dessert wine for a few hours, then layer it on top of cake and ice cream. What could be easier?

Slice or halve the fruit, place in a glass pan and drizzle the wine over the fruit. Cover and refrigerate for a few hours. Slice the cake, place a scoop of ice cream on top, ladle the marinated fruit over the top. Serve immediately.

6 ripe peaches, nectarines, or any other fruit

1 sponge or pound cake, cut into medium-sized slices

Vanilla ice cream

White dessert wine, such as Symphony or Late Harvest Riesling

Photo by Jeri Boe

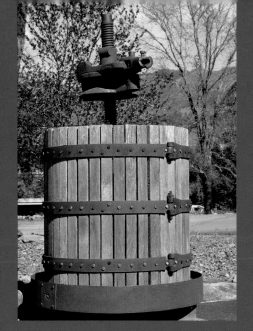

Wine Country Memorabilia

DID YOU KNOW?

As early as 1867, French experts proclaimed that California wines were "good enough" to compete with the wines of Europe, which were expensive to import. In 1900 many American wines won medals at the 1900 Paris Exposition, including wines from California, New Jersey, New York, Ohio, and Virginia.

Hermann, Missouri was the site for the first real commercial winemaking. California took the lead in the latter nineteenth century, helped along by the railroads that made it possible to ship wines back east.

The first resident of the White House to serve American wine at a state dinner was Mrs. Abraham Lincoln. The year was 1860.

WHAT TO DO WITH ALL THOSE CORKS?

These projects are fast, fun, and easy, and are an alternate to the typical cork bulletin boards. Shadow boxes are a great gift for someone who has shared your wine and quilting adventures. These would make perfect display cases for miniature quilts, wine labels, photos, and, depending on the size of the shadow box frame you purchase, can also be a place to display maps, wine tasting notes, and so on.

SHADOW BOXES WITH A TWIST

MATERIALS

Shadow box in any size from a frame or mail-order store

Lots of corks

White glue

Pencil

Paper plate or recycled container for glue

ASSEMBLY

1. Take apart the shadow box and remove the back panel.

2. Draw horizontal lines approximately ¼"–½" away from the edges of the back panel, spaced 2" apart down the length of the back panel as a guide for placement of the corks.

3. Pour a small amount of glue onto the paper plate or container. Dip the less-interesting side of each cork into the glue leaving a thin line of glue on the cork.

4. Place corks on the panel. The corks in the sample were glued in vertical groups of 3, alternating with horizontal groups of 2–3. Glue the corks one row at a time, using the pencil lines as a guide.

5. Continue gluing corks to the back panel until it is covered. Cover with plastic wrap or wax paper, and place a heavy book on top to add pressure while drying.

6. Replace the back panel in the shadow box and decorate with your favorite keepsakes.

CORK CRITTERS

These little guys make a wonderful project you can share with your children on a rainy day. All it takes are some corks, toothpicks, a long nail or metal or bamboo skewer, and whatever decorative accessories you have on hand: googly eyes from a craft store, feathers, yarn, or beads. Be creative and have fun!

1. Pierce the end of each cork with the metal skewer (an adult should do this part). You may need to cut corks in half or quarters for parts like feet or heads. An adult definitely should do the cutting.

2. Push toothpicks into the ends of the corks, depending on what you are making (older kids can handle this part).

3. Create your critter by linking the parts with the ends of the toothpicks.

4. Decorate!

A Classic Pairing:
Peanut Butter and Jelly

Finished Quilt Size: 24" x 18"

Machine appliquéd and quilted by Cyndy and Zana Rymer

Grapes aren't grown just for wine! Concord grapes were grown before the Civil War, developed by a teetotaler from Concord, Massachusets. As a New Jersey dentist with the last name of Welch discovered, they make great juice, too. Not to mention jellies, jams, and candies.

Cyndy's daughter Zana drew this quilt's design on a napkin during a post-softball dinner. In just a few hours on Mother's Day it was put together—a great way to celebrate a budding quilting relationship.

This quilt was made like a PB&J sandwich: Layers of fabric are the bread, and the fusible web the peanut butter holding it all together. An adult or older child can cut and fuse the layers of fabric, while younger children can draw and add the happy faces on the grapes and peanuts. Make it as a wallhanging for the kitchen, or as an oversized placemat (cover with plastic, available by the yard at most fabric stores).

FABRIC REQUIREMENTS

Tan: ½ yard for background

Off-white or other color: scrap about 13" square for plate

White: scraps for bread

Golds: ⅛ yard of 4–5 different fabrics, larger scraps for the peanut butter jar and crust of bread

Purples: ⅛ yard of 4–5 different fabrics, larger scrap for the jelly jar

Gold and purple tulle or other transparent fabric: small scraps

Backing and binding: ⅞ yard

Batting: 28" x 22"

Fusible web: ½ yard

Tear-away stabilizer: small pieces

Cardboard or index cards for templates

Threads to match fabrics

Decorative thread or yarn for couching on plate

Invisible thread

Permanent black marker

Fabric glue stick

CUTTING

Tan: Cut a rectangle 20½" x 14".

Gold: Cut 1 strip 2½"-wide x width of the fabric from two of the gold fabrics, or cut 2½" x 2½" squares from scraps. You need a total of 19 squares for the border.

Purple: Cut 1 strip 2½"-wide x width of the fabric from two of the purple fabrics, or cut 2½" x 2½" squares from scraps. You need a total of 19 squares for the border.

Backing: Cut a rectangle 28" x 22".

QUILT ASSEMBLY

1. Center and fuse 4" square pieces of fusible web to the wrong side of a variety of 4½" square scraps of gold and purple fabrics for the grapes and peanuts. Leave the paper backing on the fabric.

2. Trace the peanut and grape patterns on page 77 onto cardboard or an index card and cut out.

3. Using the peanut pattern, trace 24 or more peanuts onto the paper backing of the fused gold fabrics. Trace about 45 grapes onto the paper backing of the purple fabrics. Cut out the peanuts and grapes and draw happy faces on them with the permanent black marker.

4. Fuse a piece of fusible web to the wrong side of the 13" square of plate fabric. Trace a circle using a dinner plate. Cut out on the line.

Optional: Use a smaller plate and a #3 pencil or chalk marker to trace a circle centered on the right side of the "plate." This is your sewing guide for the decorative thread that is used later.

5. Enlarge the peanut butter and jelly jars and the two bread shapes (white for bread, tan for crust) 125%. Trace onto the fusible web and cut out just slightly outside the line. Fuse onto the fabrics chosen for each shape.

6. Place the plate in the center of the background tan rectangle and fuse. Fuse the bread shapes together, then fuse onto the plate.

7. Fuse the peanut butter and jelly jars onto the background. Randomly place the peanuts and grapes on top of their respective jars and onto the quilt top, and fuse in place.

Optional: Cut small pieces of tulle or other transparent fabric and use a little dab of fabric glue to tack in place over the grapes and peanuts in the jars to make it look like a full jar.

8. Using invisible thread on top and regular thread in the bobbin, zigzag stitch to couch the decorative thread onto the outer rim of the plate, then to the inner circle drawn in Step 4.

9. Use a satin stitch to cover the raw edges of the jars and bread.

10. Trim to 14½" x 20½".

You meet fun people, and dogs, at wineries

BORDER

1. Alternating gold and purple strips, sew together one set of four strips. You can also piece the borders from 2½" x 2½" squares. You need 7 squares for the side borders, and 12 squares for the top and bottom borders. Press the seams in one direction.

2. If you are using strips, cut the joined strips into 2½" units. Sew two units together end to end. Remove one square to make a side border of 7 squares. Press. Repeat to make the second side border.

Sew three units together to make the top and bottom borders of 12 squares each.

3. Sew the side borders, then the top and bottom borders, to the quilt top.

FINISHING

Refer to the Quilting Basics on pages 78–79.

1. Layer the quilt top, batting, and backing. Baste; quilt basting spray works well for small projects such as this quilt.

2. Trim the excess batting and backing. Square up the quilt to approximately 24" x 18".

3. Stitch in-the-ditch around all of the shapes, and echo-quilt one row around the first line of stitching. Stitch around the peanuts and grapes in the jars. Stipple quilt the remaining background.

4. Bind or finish as desired.

5. Attach a label to the back of the quilt, sign and date.

6. Have a PB&J to celebrate!

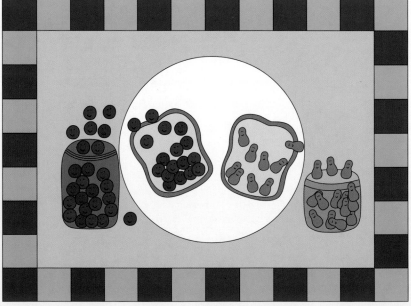

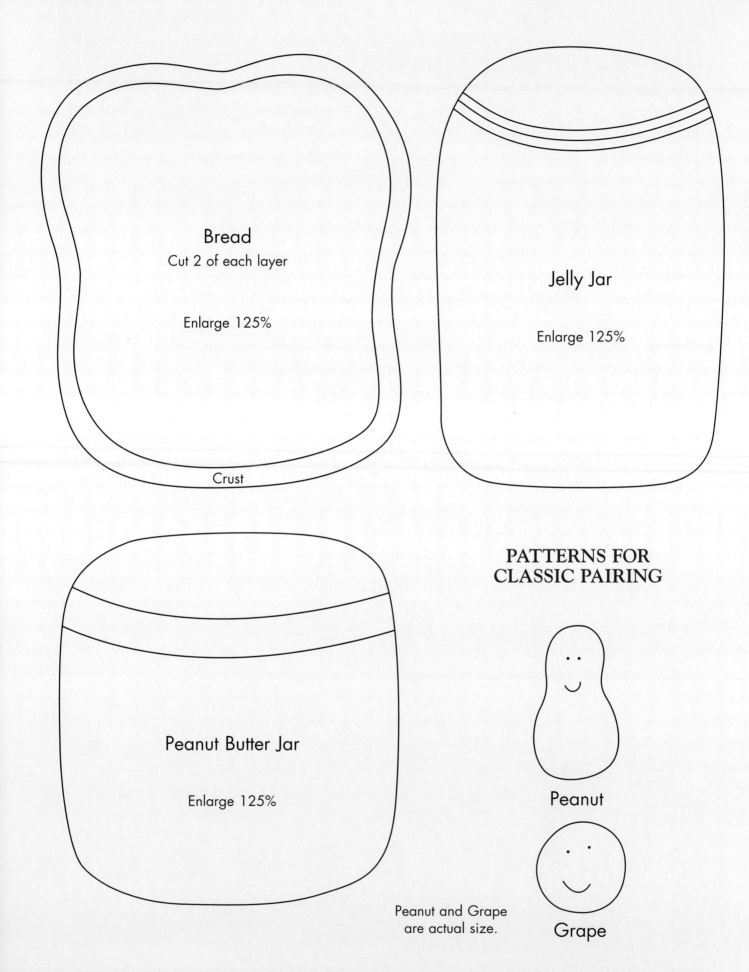

Bread
Cut 2 of each layer

Enlarge 125%

Crust

Jelly Jar

Enlarge 125%

Peanut Butter Jar

Enlarge 125%

PATTERNS FOR CLASSIC PAIRING

Peanut

Grape

Peanut and Grape
are actual size.

QUILTING BASICS

Fabric requirements are based on a 42"-width; many fabrics shrink when washed, and widths vary by manufacturer.

In cutting instructions, strips are generally cut on the crosswise grain.

GENERAL GUIDELINES

Seam Allowances
A ¼" seam allowance is used for most projects. It's a good idea to do a test seam before you begin sewing to check that your ¼" is accurate.

Pressing
In general, press the seams toward the darker fabric. Press lightly in an up-and-down motion. Avoid using a very hot iron or over-ironing, which can distort shapes and blocks.

Borders
When borders strips are cut on the crosswise grain, diagonally piece the strips together to achieve the needed lengths.

Butted Borders
In most cases, the side borders are sewn on first. When you have finished the quilt, measure it through the center vertically. This will be the length to cut the side borders. Place pins at the centers of all four sides of the quilt, as well as in the center of each side border strip. Pin the side borders to the quilt top first, matching the center pins. Using a ¼" seam allowance, sew the borders to the quilt and press.

Measure horizontally across the center of the quilt including the side borders. This will be the length to cut the top and bottom borders. Repeat, pinning, sewing, and pressing.

Backing
Plan on making the backing a minimum of 2" larger than the quilt top on all sides. Prewash the fabric, and trim the selvages before you piece.

To economize, you can piece the back from any leftover fabrics or blocks in your collection.

Batting
The type of batting to use is a personal decision; consult your local quilt shop. Cut batting approximately 2" larger on all sides than your quilt top.

Layering
Spread the backing wrong side up and tape the edges down with masking tape. (If you are working on carpet you can use T-pins to secure the backing to the carpet.) Center the batting on top, smoothing out any folds. Place the quilt top right side up on top of the batting and backing, making sure it's centered.

Basting
For machine quilting, pin-baste the quilt layers together with safety pins placed a minimum of 3"–4" apart. Start pinning in the center and move toward the edges first in vertical, then horizontal, rows.

For hand quilting, baste the layers together with thread using a long needle and light-colored thread. Knot one end of the thread. Begin stitching in the center and move out toward the edges.

Quilting

Quilting, whether by hand or machine, enhances the pieced or appliqué design of the quilt. You may choose to stitch-in-the-ditch, echo the pieced or appliqué motifs, use patterns from quilting design books and stencils, or do your own free-motion quilting. Suggested quilting patterns are included in some of the projects.

Binding

Double-Fold Straight Grain Binding (French Fold)

For a ¼" finished binding, cut the strips 2–2½" wide and piece together with a diagonal seam to make a continuous binding strip. Press the seams open, then press the entire strip in half lengthwise with wrong sides together. With raw edges even, pin the binding to the edge of the quilt a few inches away from the corner, and leave the first few inches of the binding unattached. Sew using a ¼" seam allowance.

Stop ¼" away from the first corner (see Step 1), backstitch one stitch. Lift the presser foot and needle. Rotate the quilt one-quarter turn. Fold the binding at a right angle so it extends straight above the quilt (see Step 2). Then bring the binding strip down even with the edge of the quilt (see Step 3). Begin sewing at the folded edge.

Step 1. Stitch to ¼" from corner.

Step 2. First fold for miter

Step 3. Second fold alignment. Repeat in the same manner at all corners.

Finishing the Binding

This is one method of finishing the binding. Fold under the beginning end of the binding strip ¼". Lay the binding strip over the beginning end. Continue stitching beyond the folded edge. Trim the excess binding. Fold the binding over the raw edges to the quilt back and hand stitch, mitering the corners.

MACHINE APPLIQUÉ USING FUSIBLE WEB

Lay the fusible web sheet paper-side up on the pattern and trace with a pencil. Trace detail lines with a permanent marker for ease in transferring to the fabric. Use paper-cutting scissors to roughly cut out the pieces. Leave at least a ¼" border around the shapes.

Following manufacturer's directions, fuse the web patterns to the wrong side of the appliqué fabric. It helps to use an appliqué-pressing sheet to avoid getting the adhesive on your iron or ironing board. Cut out the pieces along the pencil line. Do not remove the paper yet.

Transfer the detail lines to the fabric by placing the piece on a lightbox or up to the window and marking the fabric. Use a pencil—the lines will be covered by thread.

Remove the paper and position the appliqué piece on your project. Be sure the web (rough) side is down. Press in place, following the manufacturer's directions.

DIRECTORY *of* QUILT SHOPS *and* WINERIES

The following is meant to be a taste, rather than a comprehensive list, of the quilt shops and wineries in the major wine-producing regions of the United States. Almost every state produces wine! Keep in mind that new stores or wineries will open, and existing ones can change names or close. Please call ahead or consult the websites before visiting. Most states have wine advisory boards or councils with knowledgeable staffers who are always happy to send brochures or answer questions. Pick up issues of the many magazines such as *Touring & Tasting*, *Wine Country Living* (formerly *Appellation*), *Wine & Spirits*, or *Wine Spectator*. Once you have chosen a destination, pack a picnic basket and hit the road!

CALIFORNIA
MENDOCINO/LAKE COUNTIES: FORT BRAGG/ MENDOCINO/CLEAR LAKE/CLOVERDALE
Quilt Stores

A little farther north than the wineries, but worth the drive:

Ocean Wave Quilts
529 Trinity St.
Trinidad 707-677-3770

Fabric Indulgence
301 N. Main St.
Fort Bragg 707-964-6365

Quilted Treasures
544 S. Main St.
Kelseyville 707-279-0324

Ocean Quilts
45156 Main St.
Mendocino 707-937-4201

Wineries
Brutacao Cellars

Christine Woods

Claudia Springs Winery

Dunnewood Vineyards

Fetzer Vineyards

Gabrielli Winery

Greenwood Ridge Vineyards

Guenoc Winery

Handley Cellars

Horne

Husch Vineyards

Jepson Vineyards

Konrad Estate Winery

Lazy Creek Vineyards

Martz Winery

Milano

Navarro Vineyards

Parducci Wine Cellars

Pepperwood Springs Vineyards

Roederer Estate (Champagne)

Scharffenberger Cellars

Steele Wines

Weibel Vineyards

Wildhurst Vineyards

Weibel Vineyards

Yorkville Cellars

Zellerbach/Estate William Baccala

NEAR THE SIERRA FOOTHILLS (EL DORADO/AMADOR/AND CALAVERAS COUNTIES): MURPHYS/PLYMOUTH/ FAIR PLAY/PLACERVILLE
Quilt Stores
(On the way north or near the wineries)

Stacy's Quilt Shop
878 Alamo Dr.
Vacaville 707-447-9000

The Unique Spool
407 Corte Majorca
Vacaville 707-448-1538

Pumpkin Seed Quilts & Textiles
1414 4th St.
San Rafael 415-453-4758

Seams Like Art
318 Georgia St.
Vallejo 707-647-1222

Country Sewing Center
9639 E. Stockton Blvd.
Elk Grove 916-685-8500

Pincushion Boutique
2827 Spafford St.
Davis 530-758-3488 (they also serve a nice tea if you call ahead)

Cloth Carousel
9 Main St.
Winters 530-795-2580

Quilter's Corner, Inc.
9792-B Business Park Dr.
Sacramento 916-366-6136

Material Girls
2617 Alta Arden Expwy.
Sacramento 916-485-4252

Goose Track Fabrics
6346 Elvas Ave.
Sacramento 916-457-9412

Meissner Sewing & Learning Center
2417 Cormorant Way
Sacramento 916-920-2121

Meissner's
8771 Elk Grove Blvd.
Elk Grove 916-686-1108

Tayo's Fabrics & Quilts
10127 Fair Oaks Blvd.
Fair Oaks 916-967-5479

The Stitching Station
1000 Sunrise Ave.
Roseville 916-773-0296

Pine Tree Fabrics & Crafts
1462 Broadway
Placerville 530-626-0445

Singing Dog Quilt Works
656 Main St.
Placerville 530-622-7396

Fabrications
826 Lincoln Way
Auburn 503-887-0555

Cabin Fever Quilt Shoppe
826 Lincoln Way
Auburn 530-885-5500

Emily Ann Quilt Shop
937 Lincoln Way
Auburn 530-889-1450

Wineries
Calaveras County
Black Sheep Winery

Chatom Vineyards

French Hill Winery

Indian Rock Vineyard

Milliaire Winery

Stevenot Winery

Amador County
Amador Foothill Winery

Cedarville Vineyard

Charles Spinetta Winery

Coyote Ridge Vineyards

Deaver Vineyards

Dobra Zemlja (in a cave)

Domaine de la Terre Rouge

Greenstone Winery

Karly Winery

Montevina Winery

Shenandoah Vineyards

Sobon Estate

Stoneridge Winery

Story Vineyards

Sutter Ridge Vineyards

Young's Vineyard

El Dorado County
Boeger Winery

Charles B Mitchell Vineyards

Cairn Canyon Winery

Firefall Vineyards

Fitzpatrick Winery & Lodge
Fleur de Lys
Gold Hill Vineyard
Granite Springs Winery
Holly's Hill Vineyards
Jodar Vineyard
Latcham Vineyards
Lava Cap Winery
Madroña Vineyards
Oakstone Winery
Perry Creek Vineyards
Renwood/Santino Winery
Sierra Vista Winery
Single Leaf Vineyards
Sogno Winery
Stone's Throw Vineyard
TKC Vineyards
Van der Vijver Estate
Venezio Vineyard & Winery
Windwalker Vineyards

NORTHERN SONOMA: RUSSIAN RIVER VALLEY/DRY CREEK /ALEXANDER VALLEY
Quilt Stores
Ben Franklin Crafts
1793 Marlow Rd.
Santa Rosa 707-539-5473

The Quilted Angel
200 G St.
Petaluma 707-763-0945

Rainbow Fabrics
50 Bolinas Rd.
Fairfax 415-459-5100

Fabrications
116 Matheson St.
Healdsburg 707-433-6243

Wineries
*Northern Sonoma
(nearest to Santa Rosa)*
Armida Winery

Belvedere Winery

Davis Bynum Winery

Dehlinger Winery

De Loach Vineyards
Hop Kiln Winery
Iron Horse Vineyards
Joseph Swan Vineyards
Kendall Jackson California Coast Wine Center
Korbel Champagne Cellars
Locals (collective tasting room)
Mark West Winery
Martinelli Vineyards
Martini and Prati Winery
Mill Creek Vineyards
Paradise Ridge Winery
Porter Creek Vineyards
Rabbit Ridge Vineyards
Rochioli Vineyards and Winery
Sebastopol Vineyards
Silver Oak Cellars
Sunce Winery
Topolos at Russian River Vineyards
Trentadue Winery
The Wine Room (a multi-winery tasting room)

Dry Creek Valley
Alderbrook Winery

Bellerose Vineyard

Dry Creek Vineyard

Ferrari-Carano Vineyards and Winery

Fritz Winery

Geyser Peak Winery

Lake Sonoma Winery

Lambert Bridge Vineyards

Mill Creek Vineyards

Lytton Springs Winery

Mazzocco Vineyards

Meeker Vineyards

Pastori Winery

J. Pedroncelli Winery

Preston Vineyards

Raymond Burr Vineyards

Quivira Vineyards
A. Rafanelli

Russian River Valley/Healdsburg
Alderbrook Winery

Alexander Valley Vineyards

Field Stone Winery

Forchini Vineyards Winery

Foppiano Vineyards

Hanna Winery

J Wine Company

Johnson's Alexander Valley Vineyards

Kendall Jackson Tasting Room

Roshambo Winery

Rodney Strong Vineyards

Seghesio Family Vineyards

Simi Winery

Windsor Vineyards Tasting Room

Alexander Valley
Alexander Valley Fruit and Trading Company (yes, they make wine, too)

Chateau Souverain

Canyon Road Cellars

Clos du Bois

De Lorimier Vineyards

Murphy-Goode Estate Winery

Sausal Winery

Simi Winery

Stryker Sonoma Winery

White Oak Vineyards

SONOMA VALLEY
Quilt Stores
Kay's Fabrics
201 West Napa St.
Sonoma 707-996-3515

Wineries
Arrowood Vineyards

Bandiera Winery

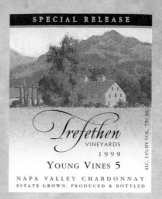

Bartholomew Park Winery
Benziger Family Carneros
B.R. Cohn
Buena Vista Winery
Chateau St. Jean Winery
Cline Cellars
Glen Ellen
Gloria Ferrer Champagne Cellars
Gundlach-Bundschu Winery
Imagery Estate Winery
Ledson Winery & Vineyards
Kenwood Vineyards
Kunde Estate Winery
Landmark Vineyards
Matanzas Creek Winery
Ravenswood Winery
Roche Winery
Rosenblum Cellars
Schug Carneros Estate
Sebastiani Vineyards
Smothers Brothers Wines
Sonoma Creek Winery
St. Francis Winery
Stone Creek Winery
Valley of the Moon Winery
Viansa Winery
Wellington Vineyards

NAPA/CARNEROS
Quilt Stores & Art Galleries
Quiltmaker
Town Center Plaza on First St.
Napa 707-252-6793

Normar Fabric & Gifts
1327 Main St.
Napa 707-253-8577—(variety of fabrics)

Art Galleries:
Jessel Gallery, 1019 Atlas Peak Rd.
Napa 707-257-2350

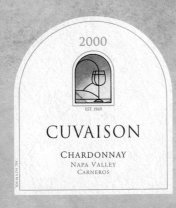

2000
Chardonnay Reserve
Cougar Ridge Vineyard

Central Coast

PRODUCED AND BOTTLED BY DOVER CANYON WINERY
PASO ROBLES, CALIFORNIA ALCOHOL 13.6% BY VOLUME

FENESTRA
2000
RESERVE
ESTATE
LIVERMORE VALLEY
SYRAH

PRODUCED AND BOTTLED BY FENESTRA WINERY
LIVERMORE, CA   ALC. BY VOL. 14.5%

Other galleries in the Napa Valley: Creative License, Gordon Huether & Partners, Imani Gallery, Karen Winograde Pottery Studio, Generations, Raku Ceramics Collection, Raspberry's Art Glass Gallery, I. Wolk Art Gallery, Spirits in Stone Gallery, Lee Youngman Galleries, Ca'Toga Galleria D'Arte

Route 29 Wineries (from south to north)

Hakusan Sake Gardens

Acacia Winery

Artesa

Domaine Carneros

Carneros Creek Winery

Codorniu Napa

Trefethen Vineyards

Rutherford Grove Winery

Newlan Vineyards and Winery

Chateau Chevre

Plam Vineyards & Winery

Domaine Chandon

Consentino Winery

Napa Cellars

Pepi Winery & Cardinale Winery

La Famiglia Winery

Hess Collection

Chateau Potelle

Vichon

Robert Mondavi

Opus One

Turnbull Wine Cellars

Cakebread Cellars

Sequoia Grove Vineyards

Supery Vineyards & Winery

Peju Province Winery

Niebaum-Coppola Estate Winery

Beaulieu (BV) Vineyard

Grgich Hills Cellars

Beaucanon Winery

Franciscan Estates

Milat Vineyards

Sullivan Vineyards Winery

Whitehall Lane Winery

Rutherford Grove Winery

Quail Ridge Cellars

Flora Springs Wine Company

V. Sattui

Heitz Wine Cellars

Edgewood Estate

Sutter Home Winery, Inc.

Louis M. Martini

Prager Winery

Merryvale Vineyards

Newton Vineyard

Beringer Vineyards

Charles Krug Winery

Markham Vineyards

Clement Vineyards

Freemark Abbey Winery

Folié a Deux Winery

Robert Keenan Winery

Smith-Madrone Vineyards

Stony Hill Vineyard

Schramsberg Vineyards

Stonegate Winery

Sterling Vineyards

Clos Pegase

Ehlers Grove

Graiser

Silverado Trail (roughly from south to north)

Monticello (not actually on the trail, but off of it)

Jarvis

William Hill

Silverado Hill Cellars

Van der Hayden

Clos du Val Wine Co.Ltd.

Signorello

Chimney Rock Winery

Regusci

Stags Leap Wine Cellars

Steltzner

Pine Ridge Winery

Silverado Vineyards

Shafer Vineyards

Robert Sinskey Vineyards

S. Anderson Vineyard

Groth Vineyards & Winery

Silver Oak Wine Cellars

Girard Winery

ZD Wines

Caymus Vineyards

Frog's Leap Winery

Napa Valley Grapevine Wreath Company (all things grapevine, no wines)

Mumm Napa Valley

Raymond Vineyards Winery

Round Hill

Wm. Harrison Vineyards

Rutherford Hill

Mario Perelli-Minetti

Joseph Phelps

Deer Park Winery

Burgess Cellars

Tudal Winery

Cuvaison

Rombauer

Dutch Henry

Clos Pegase

Traulsen Vineyards

Vincent Arroyo Winery

Chateau Montelena

Robert Pecota Winery

Bay Area: Livermore, San Jose, and South Santa Clara Quilt Stores

New Pieces Shop & Gallery
1597 & 1605 Solano Ave.
Berkeley 510-527-6779

Stonemountain & Daughter Fabrics
2518 Shattuck Ave.
Berkeley 510-845-6106

Poppy Fabric
5151 Broadway
Oakland 510-655-5151

Silk Road Fabric
272 14th St.
Oakland 510-763-1688

Quilt Fans
1716 Lincoln Ave.
Alameda 510-749-6717

Mendel's Far-out Fabrics
1556 Haight St.
San Francisco 415-621-1287

Black Cat Quilts
2608 Ocean Ave.
San Francisco 415-337-1355

Cotton Patch
1025 Brown Ave.
Lafayette 925-284-1177

ThimbleCreek
1536 Newell Ave.
Walnut Creek 925-946-9970

The Village Quilt Shop
1989 F Santa Rita Rd.
Pleasanton 925-462-9340

In Between Stitches
2033 Railroad Ave.
Livermore 925-371-7064

Going to Pieces
1375 Blossom Hill Rd. #57
San José 408-723-4133

San José Museum of Quilts and Textiles
110 Paseo de San Antonio
San José 408-971-0323

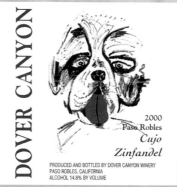

Fabrics 'n' Fun
10 S. Abbott Ave.
Milpitas 408-946-3860

Golden State Sewing Center
2435 South Winchester Blvd.
Campbell 408-866-1181

The Granary
1326 S. Mary Ave.
Sunnyvale 408-735-9830

Carolea's Knitche
586 S. Murphy Ave.
Sunnyvale 408-736-2800

Eddie's Quilting Bee
264 Castro St.
Mountain View 650-969-1714

The Laurel Leaf
648 Laurel St.
San Carlos 650-591-6790

Whiffle Tree Quilts
10261 DeAnza Blvd.
Cupertino 408-255-5270

Wineries
Livermore
Cedar Mountain Winery

Chouinard Vineyards

Concannon Vineyard

Elliston Vineyards

Fenestra Winery

Iván Tamás Winery

Little Valley Vineyard

Livermore Valley Cellars

Murietta's Well

Retzlaff Vineyards

Rios-Lovell Winery

Stony Ridge Winery

Thomas Coyne Winery

Wente Vineyards and Restaurant

White Crane Winery

San José/Morgan Hill
J. Lohr

Mirassou

Emilio Guglielmo Winery

Pedrizzetti Winery

Sycamore Creek Vineyards

Kirigin Cellars

Live Oaks

Fortino Winery

Hecker Pass

Live Oaks Winery

Thomas Kruse Winery

Solis Winery

Rapazzini Winery

Santa Cruz
Quilt Stores
Judy's Sewing Center
222 G. Mount Hermon Rd.
Scotts Valley 831- 440-1050

Hart's Fabric
1620 Seabright Ave.
Santa Cruz 831-423-5434

Cabrillo Sewing Center
1475 41st Ave. #A1
Capitola 831-462-3930

Creative Friends Craft Supplies
191 San Felipe Rd.#M1
Hollister 831-636-7773

Wineries
Obester Winery

Ridge Vineyards

Sunrise Winery

Mariani Winery

Mirassou Champagne Cellars

Ahlgren Vineyard

David Bruce Winery

Byington Winery

Roudon-Smith

Hallcrest Vineyards/Organic
Wine Works

Bonny Doon

Roudon-Smith

Soquel

BargettoWinery

Devlin Wine Cellars

Storrs Winery

MONTEREY: PACIFIC GROVE/ CARMEL VALLEY/ SALINAS COUNTY
Quilt Stores
Back Porch Fabrics
157 Grand Ave. at Central
Pacific Grove 831-375-4453

The Hand Maden
620 Lighthouse Ave.
Pacific Grove 831-373-5353

Wineries
Salinas Valley
Chalone Vineyards

Jekel Vineyards

Paraiso Springs Vineyards

Smith & Hook/Hahn Estates

Carmel Valley/Monterey
A Taste of Monterey

Ventana /Meador Estate

The Monterey Vineyard

Bernardus Winery

Galante Vineyard

Joullian Vineyards

Heller Estate/Durney Vineyards

Robert Talbott Vineyards

Chateau Julien

River Ranch Vineyards

Scheid Vineyards

CENTRAL COAST: PASO ROBLES/CAMBRIA/SAN LUIS OBISPO/EDNA VALLEY
Quilt Stores
Quilter's Cupboard
5275 El Camino Real
Atascadero 805-466-6996

The Country Sampler
5880 Traffic Way
Atascadero 805-466-7282

The Cotton Ball
475 Morro Bay Blvd.
Morro Bay 805-772-2646

Quiltin' Cousins
330 Pomeroy Ave.
Pismo Beach 805-773-4988

The Quilt Attic
106 Bridge St.
Arroyo Grande 805-474-0717

Creative Patches House
136A Thompson Rd.
Nipomo 805-929-3704

Sophie Ann's Quilts
1765-B S. Broadway
Santa Maria 805-925-1888

Wineries
Paso Robles
Adelaida Cellars

AJB Vineyards

Arciero Winery

Caparone Winery

Carmody McKnight Estate Wines

Casa de Caballos

Castoro Cellars

Creston Vineyards

Dark Star Cellars

Dover Canyon

Dunning Vineyard

Eberle Winery

EOS Estate Winery at Arciero Vineyards

Fratelli Perata

Grey Wolf Cellars

Harmony Cellars

Hidden Mountain Ranch Winery

Justin Winery

Laura's Vineyard

Live Oak Vineyards

Mastantuono

Midnight Cellars

Mission View Estate

Norman Vineyards

Peachy Canyon Winery

Pesenti Winery & Vineyards

Poalillo Vineyards

Silver Horse Winery

Sylvester Winery

Tobin James

Treana Winery

Twin Hills Ranch Winery

Wild Horse Winery

Windward Wineyard

York Mountain Winery

SAN LUIS OBISPO/EDNA VALLEY/ARROYO GRANDE
Corbett Canyon Vineyards

Claiborne & Churchill

Cottonwood Canyon Vineyard & Winery (tasting room in San Luis Obispo)

Domaine Alfred

Edna Valley Vineyard

Kynsi Winery

Laetitia Vineyard & Winery

Laverne Vineyards

Meridian Vineyards

Seven Peaks

Talley Vineyards

Windemere/Cathy MacGregor Wines

SANTA BARBARA/ SANTA YNEZ VALLEY Quilt Stores
Rasmussen's
1697 Copenhagen Dr.
Solvang 800-669-6636

Heartwarmers' Mercantile
310 E. Matilija
Ojai 805-640-1187

Blue Island Quilts
5140 Hollister Ave.
Santa Barbara 805-683-0112

The Treasure Hunt
919 Maple Ave.
Carpinteria 805-684-3360

Between Santa Barbara and San Diego
Brownie's Basement
866 E. Main St.
Santa Paula 805-525-4556

The Posie Patch
475 Channels Islands Blvd.
Port Hueneme 805-984-8818

Crazy Ladies & Friends
2451 Santa Monica Blvd.
Santa Monica 310-828-3122

Sewing Arts Center
3306 Pico Blvd.
Santa Monica 310-450-4300

Fabric Well
3075 Saviers Rd.
Oxnard 805-486-7826

Luella's Quilt Basket
1840 N. Sepulveda Blvd.
Manhattan Beach 310-545-3436

The Cotton Shop
1922 Artesia Blvd.
Redondo Beach 310-376-3518

Corner Store Quilts
4470 Cerrito Ave.
Los Alamitos 714-226-9647

Treadleart
25834 Narbonne Ave.
Lomita 310-534-5122

Piecemakers Country Store
1720 Adams Ave.
Costa Mesa 714-641-3112

Tall Mouse Arts & Crafts
23932 Aliso Creek Rd.
Laguna Niguel 949-360-5777

(See Listings for San Diego also)

Wineries
Andrew Murray Winery

Arthur Earl

Babcock Vineyards

Beckman Vineyards

Bedford Thompson Winery & Vineyard

Bernat Vineyards & Winery

Blackjack Ranch Vineyards

The Brander Vineyard/Domaine Santa Barbara

Bridlewood Winery

Buttonwood Farm Winery

Byron Vineyard & Winery

Cambria

Chimere

Cottonwood Canyon Vineyard & Winery

Curtis Winery

Epiphany Cellars

Fess Parker Winery & Vineyard

Firestone Vineyard

Foley Estates Vineyard & Winery

Foxen Vineyard

Gainey Vineyard

Daniel Gehrs Wines

Hitching Post Wines

Io

Jaffurs Wine Cellars

Kahn Winery

Koehler Winery

Lafond Winery & Vineyards

LinCourt Vineyards

Richard Longoria Wines

Los Olivos Vintners

McKeon-Phillips

Melville Winery

Mission Meadow Winery

Morovino

Mosby Winery & Vineyards

Rancho Sisquoc Winery

Richard Longoria Wines

Rideau Vineyard

Rusack Vineyards

Sanford Winery & Vineyards

Santa Barbara Winery

Sunstone Vineyards & Winery

Zaca Mesa Winery

TEMECULA VALLEY/SAN DIEGO Quilt Stores (from north to south)
Woerth Stitching
28780 Old Town Front St. #D2
Temecula 909-693-3213

Quilter's Cottage
129 S. Vine St.
Fallbrook 760-723-3060

Wineries
Temecula
Baily Vineyard & Winery

Callaway Vineyard & Winery

Churon Winery

Cilurzo Vineyard & Winery

Falkner Winery

Filsinger Vineyards & Winery

Hart Winery

Keyways Vineyard & Winery

Maurice Car'rie Winery

Mount Palomar Winery

Stuart Cellars

Thornton Winery

Van Roekel Vineyards & Winery

Wilson Creek Winery

SAN DIEGO
Quilt Stores

Fat Quarters Quilt Shop
728 Escondido Ave.
Vista 760-758-8308

Sew Special
777 E. Vista Way
Vista 760-940-0363

Rosie's Calico Cupboard
7151 El Cajon Blvd. Suite F
San Diego 619-697-5758

Sew Much Better
1824-A Oceanside Blvd.
(Boney's Center)
Oceanside 760-433-5151

Sowing Sisters
2956 Roosevelt St. Suite 1
Carlsbad 760-720-7397

Quilter's Paradise
2253 E. Valley Pkwy.
Escondido 760-738-9677

Wineries

Belle Marie Winery

Bellefleur Winery

Bernardo Winery

Broquer Vineyards

Codarossa Winery

Deer Park Winery

Fallbrook Winery

Ferara Winery

Galeano Winery

Menghihi Winery

Orfila Vineyards & Winery

Plateau Vineyards

Schwaesdall Winery

Shadow Mountain vineyards

Walter Best Winery

Witch Creek Winerty

OREGON
COASTAL QUILT STORES

The quilt shops along the coast outnumber the one winery near Lincoln City: Flying Dutchman Winery in Otter Rock.

Consult a map to find routes that will take you east toward the wineries that are just a little farther inland in the Willamette Valley.

Quilt Stores
(listed roughly north to south)

Northwest Stitchin's
926 E. Harbor St.
Warrenton 503-861-0107

Center Diamond
1065 S. Hemlock St.
Cannon Beach 503-436-0833

Creative Fabrics
475 Hwy. 101
Wheeler 503-368-5900

Jane's Fabric Patch
1110 Main Ave.
Tillamook 503-842-9392

BJ's Fabrics and Quilts
38105 Hwy. 101 South
Cloverdale 503-392-6195

Seams Sew Right Quilt Shoppe
3203 SW Hwy.10
Lincoln City 541-994-6919

Newport Quilt & Gift Company
644 SW Coast Hwy.
Newport 541-265-3492

Jodi's Quilts & Fabrics
5045 Hwy. 101
Florence 541-997-3293

Threads That Bind
120 Central Ave.
Coos Bay 541-267-0749

Forget-Me-Knots
125 Baltimore Ave.
Bandon 800-347-9021

Quilter's Corner
335 W. 7th St.
Port Orford 541-332-0502

Quilt Stores

Main Street Cloth & Mercantile
231 E. Main St.
Forest Grove 503-849-1891

Furever Friends Quilt Shop
2257 NE Cornell Rd.
Hillsboro 503-640-1907

StoryQuilts.com
9340 SW Beaverton-Hillsdale Hwy.
Beaverton 503-384-0185

Patchwork Peddlers
4107 NE Tillamook St.
Portland 503-287-5987

Daisy Kingdom
134 NW Davis St.
Portland 503-222-9033

Fibers in Motion
7855 SW Capitola Hwy.
Portland 503-977-2758

Fabric Depot
700 SE 12th Ave.
Portland 503-252-9530

Fanno Creek Calicos
12192 SW Scholls Ferry Rd.
Tigard 503-579-7977

The Quilt Block
16064 SW Tualatin-Sherwood Rd.
Sherwood 503-625-1040

The Pine Needle
429 First St.
Lake Oswego 503-635-1353

A Common Thread
16925 SW 65th Ave.
Lake Oswego 877-915-6789

Paradise Quilts & Fabrics
38821 Proctor Blvd.
Sandy 503-668-3106

The Quilting B
15410 SE 94th Ave.
Clackamas 503-656-2999

The Quilt Shoppe
1795 Willamette Falls Dr.
West Linn 503-722-7430

Country Dry Goods
248 NW 1st Ave.
Canby 503-263-3563

Jacob's House Quilt Shop
21641 Main St. NE
Aurora 503-678-3078

Boersma's
203 E. 3rd St.
McMinnville 503-472-4611

Greenbaum's Quilted Forest
240 Commercial St. NE
Salem 503-363-7973

Grandma's Attic Sewing Emporium
167 SW Court St.
Dallas 503-623-0451

The Quilt Loft
126 Ferry St. SW
Albany 541-928-7242

JanniLou Creations
1243 Main St.
Philomath 541-929-3795

Quiltwork Patches
209 SW 2nd St.
Corvallis 541-752-4820

Strawberry Patches Quilt Shop
824 Main St.
Lebanon 888-610-7779

Quilter's Junction
595 Ivy St.
Junction City 877-998-2289

The Quilt Patch
23 E. 28th St.
Eugene 541-484-1925

Aunt B's Fabrics
447 W. 11th Ave.
Eugene 541-343-9296

27th Street Fabrics
2710 Willamette St.
Eugene 541-345-7221

Foxfire Farm Quilt and Gift Shoppe
49209 McKenzie Hwy.
Vida 541-822-1011

Something to Crow About
4227 C Main St.
Springfield 541-746-3256

Ben Franklin Craft & Frame Shop
1028 Harlow Rd.
Springfield 541-726-2641

The Stitchin' Post
311 W. Cascade
Sisters 541-549-6061

Country Lady Quilt Shop
and Gallery
611 SE Jackson St.
Roseburg 541-673-1007

Seams Like Old Times Quilt Studio
2240 Stewart Pkwy.
Roseburg 541-672-5396

Plaza Sewing Center
311 SE 6th St. (Golden Rule Plaza)
Grants Pass 541-479-5757

Calico Junction
1310-C Center Dr.
Medford 541-770-8001

Grandma Dee's Fabrics,
Quilts & Stitchery
4918 Crater Lake Ave.
Medford 541-608-2874

QuiltZ
293 E. Main St.
Ashland 541-488-1650

North Willamette Wineries

Amity Vineyards (tastings at the Oregon Wine Tasting Room in McMinnville)

Argyle Winery

Beaux Freres

Bethel Heights Vineyard

Champoeg Wine Cellars

Chateau Benoit

Chateau Bianca

Chehalem

Cooper Mountain Vineyards

Cristom Vineyards

Cuneo Cellars

David Hill Vineyard

Domaine Drouhin

Domaine Serene Winery & Vineyards

Duck Pond Cellars

Dundee Springs/Perry Bower Vineyard

Edgefield Winery

Elk Cove Vineyard

Eola Hills Wine Cellars

Erath Vineyards

Eyrie Vineyards

Flynn Vineyards

Hamacher Wines

Hauer of the Daun

Helvetia Winery & Vineyard

Honeywood Winery

Kramer Vineyards

Kristin Hill Winery

Lange Winery

Laurel Ridge Winery

Lion Valley Vineyards

Marash Red Barn

Marquam Hill Vineyards

Momokawa Saké Kura

Montinore Vineyards

Oak Knoll Winery

Oregon Wine Tasting Room

Patricia Green Cellars (formerly Autumn Wind Vineyard)

Ponzi Vineyards

Redhawk Vineyard

Rex Hill Vineyards

Shafer Vineyard Cellars

Sokol Blosser Winery

Josef's Winery

Stangeland Vineyards & Winery

Tempest Vineyards

The Tasting Room

Torii Mor

Tualatin Estate Vineyards

Van Duzer Vineyards

Westrey

WillaKenzie Estate

Willamette Valley Vineyards

Wine Country Farm Cellars

Witness Tree Vineyard

Yamhill Valley Vineyards

Youngberg Hill Vineyards (by appointment)

South Willamette Valley

Airlie Winery

Benton-Lane Winery

Chateau Lorane

Hinman Vineyards/Silvan Ridge

King Estate Winery

LaVelle Vineyards

Secret House Vineyards

Springhill Cellars

Tyee Wine Cellars

Umpqua Valley

Abacela Vineyards & Winery

Callahan Ridge Winery

Champagne Creek Cellars

Girardet Wine Cellars

Henry Estate Winery

La Garza Cellars & Gourmet Kitchen

Rogue Valley

The Academy

Ashland Vineyards

Bear Creek Winery

Bridgeview Vineyards

Foris Vineyards Winery

Paschal Winery & Vineyard

Valley View Winery

Weisinger's of Ashland

Columbia River/Walla Walla

Flerchinger Vineyards

Hood River Vineyards

Coastal Wineries

Flying Dutchman Winery

Brandy Peak Distillery

Washington
Olympic Peninsula

Quilted Strait
111 N. Oak St.
Port Angeles 360-457-4733

Quilt Quarters
221 W. 1st St.
Port Angeles 360-452-6899

The Stitching Heron
126 E. Washington St.
Sequim 360-582-1230

Seaport Fabrics
2427 Sims Way
Port Townsend 360-385-3992

Quilter's Cove
1010 Water St.
Port Townsend 360-385-4254

Wineries

Bainbridge Island Vineyards & Winery

Black Diamond Winery

Fair Winds Winery

Olympic Cellars/Neuharth Winery

Greater Puget Sound/ Woodinville/Seattle Quilt Stores

Calico Country
1722 Front St.
Lynden 360-354-4832

Enchanted Needle
Lopez Village
Lopez Island 360-468-2777

Gathering Fabric
14450 Woodinville Redmond Rd.
Woodinville/Redmond
425-402-9034

Quilt Basket
2112 Yew St.
Bellingham 360-734-7080

Quilt Shop
820 Commercial Ave.
Anacortes 360-293-2146

La Conner Quilt Museum
703 S. 2nd St.
La Conner 360-466-4288

Calico Creations
400 S. 1st St.
Mt. Vernon 360-336-3241

Quilting by the Sea
221 Second St. #6
Langley 360-221-8171

Quilt with Ease
3122 Broadway
Everett 425-259-6579

The Calico Basket
4114 198th St. SW
Lynnwood 425-774-6446

Seattle Area Quilt Stores

Aunt Mary's Quilt Shop
3323 169th Place NE, Suite D
Arlington 360-657-1116

Ben Franklin Crafts
15756 Redmond Way
Redmond 425-883-2050

Quiltworks Northwest
145 106th Ave. NE
Bellevue 425-453-6005

Rochelle's Fine Fabrics
1700 Mile Hill Dr.
Port Orchard 360-895-1515

Undercover Quilts from the U.S.A.
1411 1st Ave. #106
Seattle 800-469-6511

In the Beginning Fabrics
8201 Lake City Way NE
Seattle 206-523-8862

The Loft, Inc.
1480 NW Gillman Blvd. #2
Issaquah 425-392-5877

Pieces
364 Renton Center Way SW
Renton 425-271-7160

Perfect Points Quilt Shop
23745 225th Way SE #103
Maple Valley 425-413-7845

Carriage Country Quilts
22214 Marine View Dr. S
Des Moines 206-878-9414

Sue's Rags Quilt Shop
1520 S. Dash Point Rd.
Federal Way 253-941-5076

Calico Cat
201 N. Auburn Way
Auburn 800-908-0885

Harbor Quilt
3607 Hunt NW
Gig Harbor 253-858-5414

Byrd's Nest Quilting
1613 E. 31st St.
Tacoma 253-274-0336

Quilts Northwest
2620 N. Proctor
Tacoma 206-756-0504

Gutcheon Patchworks
917 Pacific Ave. #305
Tacoma 253-383-3040

Comfy Quilts
3617 Bridgeport Way Suite F
Tacoma 253-565-5745

The Quilt Barn
1206 E. Main
Puyallup 253-845-1532

Pieces of the Past Quilts
4701 230th Ave.
Buckley 253-862-0892

Country Quilts
2723 Green River Ct.
Enumclaw 360-825-8551

Gee-Gee's Quilts
601 Yelm Ave. W
Yelm 360-458-5616

Quilter's Quarters
100 Ruby St. SE
Tumwater 360-236-0596

Sue's Stitch in Time
927 W. Railroad Ave.
Shelton 360-427-6164

Wineries
Chateau Ste. Michelle
Chatter Creek
DiStefano Winery
Facelli Winery
Firesteed Cellars
Hoodsport Winery
Market Cellar Winery
San Juan Vineyards
Sheridan Vineyard
Silver Lake Winery
Soos Creek Wine Cellars
Stimson Lane Vineyards & Estates

SOUTHWEST/COLUMBIA GORGE
Quilt Stores
Momma Made It
2035 9th Ave.
Longview 360-636-5631

Heirloom Stitches
1414 Commerce Ave.
Longview 360-425-7038

Cottons
316 E. Main St.
Vancouver 360-666-0366

Works of Heart
10706 NE 32nd Ct.
Vancouver 360-574-9053

Quilt-N-Stitch
808 SE Chkalov Dr. #3
Vancouver 360-882-9101

The Quilter
1700 SE 163rd Pl.
Vancouver 509-575-7569

Wineries
Cascade Cliffs Vineyard
Columbia Gorge
McCrea Cellars
Maryhill Winery
Rainey Valley Winery
Salishan Vineyards
Widgeon Hill Winery
Wind River Cellars

CENTRAL
Quilt Stores
Columbia Basin Quiltworks
122 W. 3rd Ave.
Moses Lake 509-764-2238

The Quilt Crossing
4 W. First Ave.
Odessa 509-982-2194

Garden Gate Quilt & Craft
1611 S. Smitty's Blvd.
Ritzville 509-659-1370

Wineries
Ryan Patrick
White Heron

YAKIMA VALLEY
Quilt Stores
Bernina Sewing Center
103 S. 7th Ave.
Yakima 360-236-0596

Quiltmania
248 Williams Blvd.
Richland 509-946-7467

Wineries
Blackwood Canyon Vintners
Bonair Winery
Chinook Wines
Eaton Hill Winery
Hinzerling Vineyards
Hogue Cellars
Hyatt Vineyards
Kestrel Wines
Kiona Vineyards Winery
Oakwood Cellars
Pontin del Roza Winery
Portteus Vineyards
Sagelands Winery
Seth Ryan Winery
Tefft Cellars
Terra Blanca
Thurston Wolfe Winery
Trey Marie Winery
Willow Crest Winery
Wineglass Cellars
Yakima River Winery

COLUMBIA VALLEY/ WALLA WALLA
Quilt Stores
Pieceable Dry Goods
5215 W. Clearwater #106
Kennewick 5098-735-6080

Fantasticks
135 Vista Way
Kennewick 509-735-3844

Suzanne's Quilt Shop at the
Walla Walla Airport 413 B
Walla Walla 509-526-9398

Quilted Heart
134 N. Grand Ave.
Pullman 509-334-7544

Quilt Shoppe
838 6th St.
Clarkston 509-751-0618

J.C. Stitching Post
N. 1601 Wenatchee Ave.
Wenatchee 509-667-0525

Columbia Valley Wineries
Badger Mountain Vineyard
Barnard Griffin
Bookwalter Winery
Claar Cellars
Columbia Crest Winery
Gordon Brothers Cellars
Marshall's Winery
Powers Winery
Preston Premium Wines
Tagaris Winery

Walla Walla Wineries
Canoe Ridge Winery
Glen Fiona
Isenhower Cellars
L'Ecole Nº·41
Maryhill Winery
Patrick M. Paul Vineyards
Seven Hills Winery
Three Rivers Winery
Walla Walla Vintners
Waterbrook Winery
Whitman Cellars
Woodward Canyon Winery

SPOKANE AREA
Quilt Stores
Bobbin Along
831 S. Main St.
Deer Park 509-276-1914

The Quilting Bee
12117 E. Mission Ave.
Spokane 509-928-6037

Sew E-Z, Too
603 W. Garland Ave.
Spokane 509-325-6644

Pacific Crescent Quilting
7454 N. Division St.
Spokane 509-484-4808

Mary Lou & Company
9116 E. Sprague St.
Spokane 509-892-1513

Kaleidoscope Quilting
1011 E. 2nd Ave.
Spokane 509-456-7375

The Buggy Barn
28848 Tramm Rd. N.
Reardon 509-796-2188

Wineries
Arbor Crest Winery

Caterina Winery

Knipprath Cellars

Latah Creek Winery

Wyvern Cellars

Northeast
Needleyn Time
9 N. Main St.
Omak 509-826-1198

Wineries
China Bend Vineyards

Gold Digger Cellars

White Heron Cellars

TEXAS
TEXAS HILL COUNTRY
Quilt Stores
The Nine Patch
307 W. Main St.
Decatur 940-627-4422

Linda's Quilt Shop
2317 E. University Dr.
Denton 940-387-7912

Stitching Post
2318 San Jacinto Blvd.
Denton 940-483-9077

Quilts & Stuff
900 NW Pkwy.
Azle 817-270-0452

Quilter's Dream
6409 Colleyville Blvd.
Colleyville 817-481-7105

Grandma Lynn's Quilts
133 N. Waco
Weatherford 817-599-4114

Cabbage Rose Quilts & Gifts
3526 W. Vickery Blvd.
Fort Worth 817-377-3993

Quilter's Stash
848 W. Pipeline Rd.
Hurst 817-595-1778

Sandy's Quilt Shop
301-B 12th St.
Joshua 817-558-2882

Waxahachie Emporium
116A N. College St.
Waxahachie 972-938-2262

Embroidery & Sewing Place
740 SW Green Oaks Blvd.
Arlington 817-467-8585

Abram House Quilt Shop
1210 W. Abram St.
Arlington 817-277-4749

Stitch 'n Time
3068 Forest Lane 104-A
Dallas 214-222-7282

Sew Quilt
7242 Fisher Rd.
Dallas 214-828-0525

Quiltmakers, Inc.
9658 Plano Rd.
Dallas 214-343-1440

Piecemaker
4951 Thunder Rd.
Dallas 214-386-9695

Needlefantasies
11407 Crestbrook Dr.
Dallas 214-363-1441

Clear Choices
2405 County Rd. 4208
Campbell 903-886-2803

Quilts on the Square
1223 Washington St.
Commerce 903-886-2299

Sew Many Quilts
101 Radio Rd. #3
Sulphur Springs 903-885-8916

Stitchin' Heaven
502 E. Goode St.
Quitman 903-763-5048

Suzy's
111 N. 6th
Garland 972-272-8180

Carriage House Quilt Shoppe
3000 Custer Rd. Suite 170
Plano 972-758-9916

Me & Mom's Quilt Shop
6942 Main St.
Frisco 972-377-7005

Quilt Country
701 S. Stemmons #260
Lewisville 972-436-7022

Rail Fence Quilt Shop
4816 Hwy. 377
Aubrey 940-440-2243

Wineries
Alamosa Wine Cellars

Becker Vineyards

Bell Mountain Vineyards

Cana Cellars Winery

Chisholm Trail Winery

Comfort Cellars Winery

Cordier Estates

Dry Comal Creek Vineyards

Fall Creek Vineyards

Flat Creek Estate

Fredericksburg Winery

Grape Creek Vineyards

Hill Country Cellars

Oberhellmann Vineyard

Pillar Bluff Vineyards

Poteet Country Winery

Sister Creek Vineyards

Slaughter-Leftwich Vineyards

Spicewood Vineyards

Texas Hills Vineyard

Wimberly Valley Winery

Woodrose Winery

NORTH CENTRAL TEXAS
Quilt Stores
Kaleidoscope Quilt Shop
303 Reast Rd.
Whitesboro 903-564-4681

Mary's Quilt Shop
1520 Texoma Pkwy.
Sherman 903-893-6277

J.J. Stitchers
612 Blanton Dr.
Sherman 903-893-9012

Bernina & Sew Much More
2400 Stillhouse Rd.
Paris 903-784-6342

One More Stitch
210 E. Henry St.
Hamilton 254-386-8874

Nancy's Quilt Block
1412 N. Valley Mills Dr.
Waco 254-776-4989

Carol's Creations
601A S. 2nd St.
Kileen 254-628-8788

A Stitch in Time
518 N. 7th
Temple 254-774-9990

Wineries
Brushy Creek Vineyards

CrossTimbers Winery

Delaney Vineyard

Duckworth Winery

Hidden Springs Winery

Homestead Winery

La Bodega Winery

La Buena Vida

Lone Oak Vineyards

North Star Winery

Pleasant Hill Winery

Tehuacana Creek Vineyards

Tejas Cellars

WEST TEXAS
Quilt Stores

The Quilt Shop
4525 50th St.
Lubbock 806-793-2485

A Stitch in Time
2305 FM 1703
Alpine 915-837-0950

Wineries

Cap*Rock Winery

Llano Estacado

Pheasant Ridge Winery

Ste. Genevieve Winery

EAST TEXAS
Quilt Stores

Grimes Sewing Center
619 W. Oak St.
Palestine 903-729-2889

Quilt Cottage
401 E. Hospital St.
Nacogdoches 409-559-7000

Polly's Quilt Cottage
3211 S. Texas Ave.
Bryan 979-775-1681

Pruitt's Fabric & Quilt Shop
318 George Bush Dr.
College Station 409-693-9357

Stitch Haven
1600 S. Day St.
Brenham 979-836-3200

Quilter's Mercantile
6311-E FM 1488
Magnolia 281-252-3550

Juliene's Quilt Shop
26303 Preston Unit B
Spring 281-355-9820

Quilt Impressions
12810 Fountain Lake Cir.
Stafford 281-240-4992

Quilt 'n Sew Studio
1841 N. Mason Rd.
Katy 281-347-0470

'N Calicoes Too
10115 Hammerly Blvd.
Houston 713-464-8358

Great Expectations Quilts
14090 Memorial Dr.
Houston 281-496-1366

Front Porch Quilts
5050 FM 1960 W. #127
Houston 281-444-2882

Creative Quilting
10804 Fallstone Ste. 220
Houston 281-879-5270

Painted Pony 'n Quilts
1015 S. Broadway
Laporte 281-471-5753

Quakertown Quilts
180 S. Friendswood Dr.
Friendswood 281-996-1756

The Fabric Store
1605 S. Hwy. 69
Nederland 409-729-5288

Wineries

Bruno & George Wines

Kiepersol Estates Vineyard

Messina-Hoff Wine Cellars

Piney Woods Country Wines

Red River Winery

SOUTH TEXAS
Wineries

Blue Mountain Vineyards

Haak Vineyards

McReynolds Wines

Val Verde Winery

MICHIGAN
NORTHERN MICHIGAN
Quilt Stores

Cousin's Quilt & Needlework
Shop 222 N. Bridge St.
Bellaire 231-533-4661

Liberty Quilt Shop
9027 S. Kasson St.
Cedar 231-228-6689

Material Girl Quilt Shop
3938 Rennie School Rd.
Traverse City 231-943-5858

Cranberry Christmas
3997 M-72E
Acme 231-938-5944

Sewing Depot
1425-C S. Airport Rd. West
Traverse City 231-946-2554

Quilts by the Lake
194 S. Benzie Blvd.
Beulah 231-882-4024

Quilted Heart
607 Parkdale Ave.
Manistee 231-723-7069

Wineries

Bel Lago Winery

Black Star Farms

Boskydel Vineyards

Chateau de Leelenau

Chateau Fontaine

Chateau Grand Traverse

Ciccone Winery

Good Harbor Vineyards

L. Mawby Vineyards

Leelenau Wine Cellars

Peninsula Wine Cellars

Raftshol Vineyards

Shady Lane Cellars

Willow Vineyard

SOUTHERN MICHIGAN
Quilt Stores

The General Store
103 E. Colby St.
Whitehall 231-894-2164

Forever Fabrics
214 S. Franklin St.
Greenville 616-225-8486

Attic Window Quilt Shop
1035 Four Mile Rd. NW
Comstock Park 616-785-3357

Smith-Owen Sewing & Quilt Center
4051 Plainfield Ave. NE
Grand Rapids 616-361-5484

Grand Quilt Co.
3605 28th St. SE
Grand Rapids 616-942-6904

Country Needleworks
584 Chicago Dr.
Jenison 616-457-9410

It's Stitching Time
150 E. Main St.
Zeeland 616-772-5525

Field's Fabrics
281 E. 8th St.
Holland 616-392-4806

Quilts Plus
4644 W. Main St.
Kalamazoo 616-383-1790

Viking Sewing Center
5401 Portage Rd.
Kalamazoo 616-342-5808

Carol's Quilt Cottage
1985 Zoschke Rd.
Benton Harbor 616-849-4065

The Silver Needle
415 State St.
St. Joseph 616-982-8521

Loving Stitches Quilt Shop
7291 Red Arrow Hwy.
Stevensville 616-465-3795

Wineries

Contessa Wine Cellars

Fenn Valley Vineyards

Heart of the Vineyard Winery

Jomagrha Winery

K. Edward Winery

Lemon Creek

Lone Oak Vineyard Estate

Peterson & Sons Winery

St. Julian Wine Company

Tabor Hill Winery & Restaurant

Tartan Hill

Warner Vineyards

MISSOURI
Quilt Stores

Quilts 'n Treasures
219 N. Main St.
Hannibal 573-248-1607

Hickory Stick
326 N. Main St.
Hannibal 573-221-4538

Sticky Wicket
101 W. Monroe St.
Mexico 573-581-6262

Homestead Hearth
105 N. Coal St.
Mexico 573-581-1966

The Fabric Shop
511 E. Spring St.
Boonville 660-882-5113

Silks & More Fine Fabrics
2541 Bernadette Dr.
Columbia 800-269-2655

Clark's Fabrics
Hwy 5 & 52 W.
Versailles 573-378-5696

Quilter's Cove
1040 Main St.
Osage Beach 573-302-9923

Patches Etc. Quilt Shop
337 S. Main
St. Charles 314-946-6004

Kalico Patch
412 Boone's Lick Rd.
St. Charles 636-946-9520

The Quilted Fox
10403 Clayton Rd.
St. Louis 314-993-1181

The Sign of the Turtle
5223 Gravois St.
St. Louis 314-351-5550

Treasured Keepsakes
1771 Parker Rd.
St. Louis 800-300-6316

Jackman's Fabrics
1000 Lincoln Hwy.
St. Louis 618-632-2700

Quilt 'N Stitch
9109 Watson Rd.
Crestwood 314-961-0909

Quilt-A-Lot Fabrics
540 E. Springfield Rd.
St. Clair 636-639-8106

The Sewing Basket
2504 William St.
Cape Girardeau 877-339-7667

Wineries
Adam Puchta Winery
Augusta Winery
Balducci Vineyards
Bias Vineyards & Winery
Blumenhop Vineyards & winery
Bristle Ridge Vineyards
Buffalo Creek Winery
Bynum Winery
Ferrigno Winery
Heinrichshaus Vineyard & Winery

Hermannhof Winery
La Dolce Vita Vineyard & Winery
Les Bourgeois Vineyards
Meramac Vineyards
Montelle Winery
Montserrat Vineyards
Mount Pleasant Winery
Native Stone Vineyard, Inc.
OakGlenn Vineyards & Winery
Peaceful Bend Vineyard
Pirtle's Weston Vineyards
Phoenix winery & Vineyards
River Ridge Winery
Röbller Vineyard Winery
Sainte Genevieve Winery
James Winery
Stone Hill Winery (Branson, Hermann, Florence)
Stonehaus Farms Winery
Sugar Creek Vineyards & Winery
Summit Lake Winery
Thornhill Vineyards Winery
Tower Rock Winery
Winery of the Little Lambs

INDIANA
NORTHERN INDIANA
Quilt Stores
Quilter's Haven
Sand Ridge Plaza Rt. 30
Dyer 219-322-4624

Bits 'N Pieces
732 N. Main St.
Crown Point 219-662-9030

Crazy Eighths
301 Grand Ave. Suite B
Chesterton 219-929-4511

Wineries
Anderson's Orchard & Winery
Dune Ridge Winery
Lake Michigan Winery

CENTRAL INDIANA
Quilt Stores
The Quilting Basket
439 E. Lincoln Rd.
Kokomo 765-865-9269

World Class Sewing
1105 S. 10th St.
Noblesville 317-776-2204

Quilt Quarters
12405 N. Meridian St.
Carmel 317-844-3636

Quiltmakers
11854 Allisonville Rd.
Fishers 317-585-5825

Needle in the Haystack
132 W. State St.
Pendleton 317-778-7936

Ruth's Legacy
104 W. High St.
Pendleton 317-778-2488

Quilts Plus
1748 E. 86th St.
Indianapolis 800-840-2241

Quilt Quarters
3137 E. Thompson Rd.
Indianapolis 317-791-1336

Wineries
Easley Winery
Ferrin's Fruit Winery
Gaia Wines
Sugar Grove Winery
Terre Vin Winery

SOUTH CENTRAL INDIANA
Quilt Stores
Ady's Fabrics & Notions
75 W. Washington St.
Morgantown 812-597-0578

Fabrix
16 W. Main St.
Bloomfield 812-384-8044

Fountain Fabrics
301 N. Morton St.
Bloomington 812-333-1335

Just Around the Block
414 W. 6th St.
Bloomington 812-333-1385

Loose Threads
205 S. Maple St.
Seymour 812-524-2013

Wineries
Brown County Winery
Butler Winery
Chateau Thomas Winery
Oliver Winery
Shadey Lake Winery
Simmons Winery

SOUTHERN INDIANA
Quilt Stores
L and L Yard Goods
1814 Taylor St.
Madison 812-273-1041

Quilter's Garden
204 Elm St.
Corydon 812-738-1357

Wineries
Chateau Pomije Winery
French Lick Winery
Huber Orchard & Winery
Kauffman Winery
Lanthier Winery
Madison Vineyards
The Ridge Winery
Thomas Family Winery
Turtle Run Winery
Villa Milan Vineyard
Winzerwald Winery

NEW YORK
LONG ISLAND
Quilt Stores
Patchworks Quilting
122 Main St.
Sayville 800-647-5596

Sentimental Stitches
181 Main St.
Cold Spring Harbor 631-692-4145

Wineries
Bedell Cellars
Bidwell Vineyards
Castello di Borghese/Hargrave
Channing Daughters
Corey Creek Vineyards
Duck Walk Vineyards
Gallucio Estate/Gristina
HargraveVineyards
Laurel Lake Vineyards
Lenz Winery
Lieb Family Cellars
Macari Vineyards
Martha Clara Vineyards
Osprey's Dominion Winery
Palmer Vineyards
Paumanok Vineyards
Peconic Bay Winery
Pelligrini Vineyards

Pindar Vineyards

Pugliese Vineyards

Raphael

Ternhaven Cellars

Wolffer Estate

FINGER LAKES
Quilt Stores

Apple Country Quilt Shop & Café
51 State St.
Holley 866-340-6100

Fabrics & Findings
50 Anderson Ave.
Rochester 585-461-2820

Patricia's Fabric House
333 W. Commercial St.
East Rochester 585-248-2362

Mendon Village Quilt Shop
1350 Pittsford-Mendon Rd.
Mendon 585-624-3130

Springlake Market & Fabrics
4219 Yates Rd.
Savannah 315-594-8485

Patchwork Plus
36 Jordan St.
Skaneateles 315-685-6979

Fabrics, etc.
71 S. Main St.
Canandaigua 585-394-6350

Amish Country Store
1190 Earls Hills Rd.
Penn Yan 315-781-2571

Quilt Room
1870 Hoyt Rd.
Penn Yan 315-536-5964

Material Rewards
10160 Sandy Hill Rd.
Dansville 585-335-2050

Cottonseed Quilting Co.
9 Charlesworth Ave.
Avoca 607-566-9264

Lake Country Patchwork
67 Shether St.
Hammondsport 607-569-3530

Wineries

Amberg Wine Cellars

Anthony Road Wine Company

Arcadian Estate Vineyards

Atwater Estate Vineyards

Barrington Cellars/Buzzard
Crest Vineyard

Bully Hill Vineyard

Casa Larga

Cascata Winery at the
Professors' Inn

Cayuga Ridge Estate Winery

Chateau Frank

Chateau LaFayette Reneau

Chateau Renaissance Wine
Cellars

Dr. Konstantin Frank's Vinifera
Wine Cellars

Earle Estates Winery & Meadery

Finger Lakes Champagne House

Fox Run Vineyards

Fulkerson Winery

Glenora Wine Cellars

Goose Watch Winery

Hazlitt 1852 Vineyards

Heron Hill Winery

Hunt Country Vineyard

Keuka Overlook Wine Cellars

Keuka Spring Vineyards

King Ferry Winery

Knapp Vineyards Winery

Lakeshore Winery

Lakewood Vineyard

Lamoreaux Landing Wine Cellars

Leidenfrost Vineyard

McGregor Vineyard Winery

Pleasant Valley Wine Company

Prejean Winery

Ravines Wine Cellar

Red Newt Cellars

Seneca Shore Wine Cellars

Sheldrake Point Vineyard & Café

Six Mile Creek Vineyard

Standing Stone Vineyards

Swedish Hill Vineryard

Thirsty Owl Wine Company

Torrey Ridge Winery

Treleaven

Wagner Vineyard

Woodbury Vineyards

PENNSYLVANIA
LAKE ERIE REGION
Quilt Stores

Calico Patch Quilt Shoppe
107 Clay St.
North East 814-725-2275

The Sewing Loft
40 N. Main St.
Union City 814-438-9007

The Quilt Square
560 Washington St.
Meadville 814-333-4383

International Fabric Collection
3445 West Lake Rd.
Erie 814-838-0740

Buy the Yard Quilt Shop
202 East 10th St.
Erie 814-454-4000

Millcreek
2421 W. 26th St.
Erie 888-836-8227

Wineries

Arrowhead Wine Cellars

Conneaut Cellars Winery

Heritage Wine Cellars

Mazza Vineyards

Penn Shore Vineyards

Wilhelm Winery

PITTSBURGH COUNTRYSIDE
Quilt Stores

Amy Baughman Sewing Center
472 Constitution Blvd.
New Brighton 724-846-8140

The Quilt Company
3940 Middle Rd.
Allison Park 412-487-9532

Quilted Cottage
690 Lincoln Ave.
Pittsburgh 412-734-5141

Piecing It Together
3458 Babcock Blvd.
Pittsburgh 412-364-2440

Wineries

Christian W. Klay Winery

C. T. Miller Vineyards

Glades Pike Winery

La Casa Narcisi

Lapic Winery Ltd.

Michael Charles Winery

Quaker Ridge Winery

Raspberry Acres

Stone Villa Wine Cellars Inc.

The Vineyard by Mellon

GROUNDHOG (CENTRAL)
Quilt Stores

Harriet's Quilt Shop
271 Philadelphia St.
Indiana 724-465-4990

The Quilt Peddler
620 Lamberd Ave.
Johnstown 814-266-5661

Wineries

Evergreen Valley Vineyards

Flickerwood Wine Cellars

Laurel Mountain Vineyard

Oak Spring Winery

Windgate Vineyards

The Winery at Wilcox

UPPER SUSQUEHANNA
Quilt Store

Our Gathering Place
936 Plaza Dr.
Montoursville 570-368-1130

Wineries

Bastress Mountain Winery

Benigna's Creek

Brookmere Farm Vineyards

Hunter's Valley Winery

Mount Nittany Vineyard & Winery

Oregon Hill Winery

Shade Mountain Winery

Susquehanna Valley Winery

LOWER SUSQUEHANNA
Quilt Stores

Smile Spinners
1975 Valley Rd.
Marysville 717-957-4225

Quilter's Gathering
5490C Derry St.
Harrisburg 717-564-4828

Calico Corner
341 Barnstable Rd.
Carlisle 717-249-8644

Ben Franklin Crafts
4880 Carlisle Pike
Mechanicsburg 717-975-0490

Quilt Odyssey
15004 Burnt Mill Rd.
Shippensburg 717-423-5148

Gettysburg Quilting Center
523 Baltimore St.
Gettysburg 800-676-2658

Needle & Thread
2215 Fairfield Rd.
Gettysburg 717-334-4011

The Quilt Patch
1897 Hanover Pike.
Littlestown 717-359-4121

Olde Tollgate Village
2547 S. Queen St.
York 717-741-0817

Ben Franklin Crafts
2541 East Market St.
York 717-755-7312

The Patchwork Dollhouse
8 Meadow Lane
Lancaster 717-569-4447

1830 House
1830 Ursinus Ave.
Lancaster 717-393-1019

Goods Store
333 W 4th St.
Curryville 717-786-9028

Zook's Fabrics
3535 Old Philadelphia Pike
Intercourse 717-768-8153

Bird-in-Hand Country Store
2679-B Old Philadelphia Pike
Bird-in-Hand 717-393-5321

Wineries
Adams County Winery

Allegro Wines

Fox Ridge Winery

Mount Hope Estate Winery

Naylor Wine Cellars

Nissley Vineyards

Seven Valleys Winery

Westhanover Winery

LEHIGH VALLEY & BUCKS COUNTY
Quilt Stores

Julie's Sewing Basket
1870 Briarcliff Terr.
Allentown 610-434-7600

The Quiltery
140 W Center St.
Nazareth 610-759-9699

Summer House Needleworks
6375 Oley Turnpike Rd.
Allentown 610-689-9090

Lynn's Quilt Shop
120 Shoemaker Rd.
Pottstown 610-718-5505

The Souder Store
357 Main St.
Souderton 215-723-2017

Martin's Country Market
Hayloft Fabrics
150 Moorview Blvd.
Morgantown 610-286-5045

Wineries
Bashore & Stoudt Country Winery

Blue Mountain Vineyards

Calvaresi Winery

Cherry Valley Vineyards

Clover Hill Vineyards & Winery

Franklin Hill Vineyards

Galen Glen Vineyards

Maiolatesi Wine Cellars

Manatawny Creek Winery

Pinnacle Ridge Winery

Slate Quarry Winery

Stoney Acres Winery

Vynecrest Winery

PHILADELPHIA COUNTRYSIDE
Quilt Stores

Gone to Pieces
325 E. Gay St.
West Chester 610-918-9101

A Patch of Country Inc.
22 Olde Village Rd.
Chadds Ford 610-459-8993

Works in Cloth
2525 Aspen St.
Philadelphia 215-236-8824

Bittersweet Designs
1116 Taylorsville Rd.
Washington Crossing
215-493-2752

The Country Quilt Shop
515 Stump Rd.
Montgomeryville 215-855-5554

Wineries
Buckingham Valley Vineyards

Chaddsford Winery

Country Creek Winery

Eagle's Crest Vineyard

Fratelli Desiato Vineyards

French Creek Ridge Vineyards

Peace Valley Winery

Rose Bank Winery

Rushland Ridge Vineyards

Sand Castle Winery

Smithbridge Cellars

VIRGINIA
NORTHERN VIRGINIA
Quilt Stores

The Quilt Patch
10381 Main St.
Fairfax 703-272-6937

Memere's Garden
201B Harrison St. SE
Leesburg 703-669-0807

Quilter's Confectionery
7333 Hunton St.
Warrenton 540-347-3631

G Street Fabrics
5077 Westfields Blvd.
Centreville 703-818-8090

G Street Fabrics
6250 Seven Corners Center
Falls Church 703-241-1700

Wineries
Breaux Vineyards

Chrysalis Vineyards

Farfelu Vineyards

Gray Ghost Vineyards

Hartwood Winery

Hidden Brook Winery

Linden Vineyards

Lost Creek Winery

Loudoun Valley Vineyards

Naked Mountain Vineyards

Oasis Vineyards

Rappahannock Cellars

Spotted Tavern Winery & Dodds
Cider Mill

Swedenburg Estate Vineyard

Tarara Vineyard & Winery

Unicorn Winery

Willowcroft Farm Vineyards

Windham Winery

EASTERN VIRGINIA
Quilt Stores

Quilter's Heaven
1000 Charles St.
Fredericksburg 540-371-9011

Sis 'N Me Quilt Shoppe
3361 Western Branch Blvd.
Chesapeake 757-686-2050

Clark & Co.
940 Unicorn Trail
Chesapeake 757-547-2039

Nancy's Calico Patch
21 Hidenwood Shopping Center
Newport News 757-596-7397

Needlecraft Corner at
Williamsburg Soap & Candle Co.
7521 Richmond Rd.
Williamsburg 757-564-3354

Quilts Unlimited
110-E S Henry St.
Williamsburg 757-253-8700

Fabric Hut
2340 E. Little Creek Rd.
Norfolk 757-588-1300

What's Your Stitch 'N Stuff
5350 Kempsriver Dr. #104
Virginia Beach 757-523-2711

Wineries
Ingleside

James River Wine Cellars

Lake Anna Winery

Oak Crest Winery

Williamsburg Winery Ltd. and
Gabriel Archer Tavern

Windy River Winery

CENTRAL (MONTICELLO)
Quilt Stores

Early Times Workshop
129-133 E. Davis St.
Culpeper 540-829-7200

Sewing Nook
182 Zan Rd.
Charlottesville 804-975-1059

Cottonwood
2039 Barracks Rd.
Charlottesville 434-244-9975

Quilts Unlimited
1023 Emmet St.
Charlottesville 804-979-8110

JoAnn Fabric and Crafts
8032 W. Broad St.
Richmond 804-270-0442

Rachel's Quilt Patch
40 Middlebrook Ave.
Staunton 540-886-7728

The Quilter's Corner
1318 Sycamore Square
Midlothian 804-794-1990

Wineries
Afton Mountain Vineyards

Autumn Hill Vineyards/Blue Ridge
Winery

Barboursville Vineyards/Palladio
Restaurant

Burnley Vineyards & Daniel
Cellars (and guest house)

Christensen Ridge Winery

Cooper Vineyards

Dominion Wine Cellars

First Colony Winery

Grayhaven Winery

Hill Top Berry Farm & Winery

Horton Cellars
Winery/Montdomaine Cellars

Jefferson Vineyards

Kluge Estate Winery & Vineyard

Mountain Cove Vineyards &
Winegarden

Oakencroft Vineyard & Winery

Old House Vineyards

Prince Michel Vineyards &
Rapidan River Vineyards

Rebec Vineyards

Rockbridge Vineyard

Rose River Vineyards & Trout Farm

Sharp Rock Vineyards

Smokehouse Winery

Stone Mountain Vineyard

Stonewall Vineyard

Veritas Winery

White Hall Vineyards

Wintergreen Winery

SOUTHWESTERN VIRGINIA
Quilt Stores
Quilting Connection
2825 Brambleton Ave.
Roanoke 540-776-0794

Fabric Mill Outlet
453 S. Main St.
Rocky Mount 540-483-2822

Quilted Expressions
3622 Old Forrest Rd.
Lynchburg 434-385-6765

Sew Biz
94 Harvey St.
Radford 540-639-1138

In Stitches
475 Arrowhead Trail
Christiansburg 540-382-1180

Wineries
Abingdon Vineyard & Winery

AmRhein Wine Cellar

Boundary Rock Farm & Vineyard

Chateau Morrisette

Dye's Vineyard

Hickory Hill Vineyards

Highlands Harvest Vineyard &
Farm Winery

Peaks of Otter Winery

Tomahawk Mill Winery

Valhalla Vineyards

Villa Appalaccia Winery

SHENANDOAH VALLEY
Quilt Stores
Patchwork Plus
17 Killdeer Lane
Dayton 540-879-2505

Rachel's Quilt Patch
40 Middlebrook Ave.
Staunton 540-886-7728

Wineries
Deer Meadow Vineyard

Guilford Ridge Vineyard

Landwirt Vineyards

North Mountain Vineyard &
Winery

Shenandoah Vineyards

WEBSITES
Chock-full of good information:

www.atime4wine.com

www.drinkwine.com

www.fingerlakeswine.com

www.hiddencellars.com

www.inidianawines.org

www.insidenapa.com

www.liwines.com

www.localwineevents.com

www.michiganwines.com

www.missouriwine.org

www.napavalley.com

www.napavinters.com

www.oregonpinotnoir.com

www.oregonwine.com

www.oregonwines.com

www.pennsylvaniawine.com

www.sonomawine.com

www.stratsplace.com (huge
collection of wine labels)

www.touringandtasting.com
(*Touring & Tasting* magazine)

www.twgga.org (Texas Wine
Growers)

www.usawines.com

www.travelenvoy.com

www.virginiawines.org

www.washingtonwine.org

www.wine.com

www.winecountry.com

www.winecountryliving.net (*Wine
Country Living* magazine online)

www.wineenthusiast.com

www.wineinstitute.com

www.wineloverspage.com

www.wineroad.com

www.wineskinny.com (very
friendly site with lots of great
reviews, wine travel tips, etc.)

www.winespectator.com

www.winetoday.com

www.yamhillwine.com

For more information about the
floorcloth shown on page 65,
contact Deb Caulo at Village
Floorcloths, Norwich, Vermont,
caulovt@aol.com.

BIBLIOGRAPHY

Allen, Max, *Red and White: Wine Made Simple*, San Francisco, CA: The Wine Appreciation Guild, 2001.

Harriet Hargrave and Sharyn Craig, *The Art of Classic Quiltmaking*, Lafayette, CA: C&T Publishing, 2000.

Mastering Machine Appliqué, 2nd ed., Lafayette, CA: C&T Publishing, 2001.

Mondavi, Robert, *Harvests of Joy*, San Diego, CA: Harcourt Brace & Company, 1998.

Joseph, Robert and Margaret Rand, *KISS Guide to Wine*, New York: Dorling Kindersley, 2000.

Laverick, Charles, ed., *The Beverage Testing Institute's Buying Guide to Wines of North America*, New York: Sterling Publishing Co., Inc., 1999.

Lukacs, Paul, *American Vintage: The Rise of American Wine*, Boston: Houghton Mifflin Company, 2000.

McInerney, Jay, *Bacchus & Me: Adventures in the Wine Cellar*, New York: The Lyons Press, 2000.

McKim, Ruby, *101 Patchwork Designs*, New York: Dover Publications, 1962.

Schaefer, Dennis, *Touring the California Wine Country*, Houston, TX: Gulf Publishing Company, 1997.

OTHER FINE BOOK *from* C&T PUBLISHING

All About Quilting from A to Z, From the Editors and Contributors of Quilter's Newsletter Magazine and Quiltmaker magazine

Appliqué Inside the Lines: 12 Quilt Projects to Embroider & Appliqué, Carol Armstrong

Block Magic, Too!: Over 50 NEW Blocks from Squares and Rectangles, Nancy Johnson-Srebro

Bouquet of Quilts, A: Garden-Inspired Projects for the Home, Edited by Jennifer Rounds & Cyndy Lyle Rymer

Contemporary Classics in Plaids & Stripes: 9 Projects from Piece 'O Cake Designs, Linda Jenkins & Becky Goldsmith

Dresden Flower Garden: A New Twist on Two Quilt Classics, Blanche Young and Lynette Young Bingham

Elm Creek Quilts: Quilt Projects Inspired by the Elm Creek Quilts Novels, Jennifer Chiaverini & Nancy Odom

Felt Wee Folk: Enchanting Projects, Salley Mavor

Hand Appliqué with Alex Anderson: Seven Projects for Hand Appliqué, Alex Anderson

Hand Quilting with Alex Anderson: Six Projects for First-Time Hand Quilters, Alex Anderson

Laurel Burch Quilts: Kindred Creatures, Laurel Burch

Luscious Landscapes: Simple Techniques for Dynamic Quilts, Joyce R. Becker

Paper Piecing Potpourri: Fun-Filled Projects for Every Quilter, From the Editors and Contributors of Quilter's Newsletter Magazine and Quiltmaker magazine

Paper Piecing with Alex Anderson: •Tips •Techniques •6 Projects, Alex Anderson

Perfect Union of Patchwork & Appliqué, A, Darlene Christopherson

Q is for Quilt, Diana McClun & Laura Nownes

Ultimate Guide to Longarm Quilting, The: •How to Use Any Longarm Machine •Techniques, Patterns & Pantographs •Starting a Business •Hiring a Longarm Machine Quilter, Linda Taylor

Radiant New York Beauties: 14 Paper-Pieced Quilt Projects, Valori Wells

Reverse Appliqué with No Brakez, Jan Mullen

Rotary Cutting with Alex Anderson: Tips, Techniques, and Projects, Alex Anderson

Shoreline Quilts: 15 Glorious Get-Away Projects, compiled by Cyndy Rymer

Show Me How to Machine Quilt: A Fun, No-Mark Approach, Kathy Sandbach

Simple Fabric Folding for Christmas: 14 Festive Quilts & Projects, Liz Aneloski

Slice of Christmas from Piece O' Cake Designs, A, Linda Jenkins & Becky Goldsmith

Start Quilting with Alex Anderson, 2nd Edition: Six Projects for First-Time Quilters, Alex Anderson

For more information, write for a free catalog:
C&T Publishing, Inc.
P.O. Box 1456
Lafayette, CA 94549
(800) 284-1114
Email: ctinfo@ctpub.com
Website: www.ctpub.com

For quilting supplies:
Cotton Patch Mail Order
3405 Hall Lane, Dept.CTB
Lafayette, CA 94549
(800) 835-4418
(925) 283-7883
Email:quiltusa@yahoo.com
Website: www.quiltusa.com

Note: Fabrics used in the quilts shown may not be currently available since fabric manufacturers keep most fabrics in print for only a short time.

INDEX

Above the Clouds (Lynn Koolish), 23–26

Arcturos Winery, 46

Art, wineries and, 59

Backing, 78

Back Porch Fabrics, 8

Bags, for wine bottles, 69

Baltimore Album Wedding Quilt (Donna Hall), 62

Basting, 78

Beautiful Mustard (Vicki Chambers), 22

Bedell Cellars, 60

Beringer Vineyards, 13

Bernardus Winery and Vineyard, 8

Bias bars, 54

Binding, 79

Blanket stitching, machine appliqué, 15

Borders, 78

Boyd, Don, 36

B.R. Cohn Winery, 5

Bruno (Darcie Kent, 12

California Colors (Mary Ellen Parsons), 9

Calistoga, CA, 13

Carmel Valley, CA, 8

Caulo, Deb, 65

Chardonnay (Jan Rashid), 32

Channing Daughters, 59

Chateau Chantal, 46

Chateau Grand Traverse, 46

Chateau Julien Wine Estate, 8

Chateau Souverain, 23

Chateau Ste. Michelle, 59

Chicken with Red Wine and Fruit, 71

Chinese Pesto, 70

Ciccone, Vineyards, 46

Classic Pairing (Cyndy and Zana Rymer), 7, 74–77

Clos du Bois, 23

Clos Pegase, 59

Colors of My Valley, The (Anni Donohue), 41

Colors of the Vineyard (Carol Armstrong), 46–51

Copia: American Center for Wine, Food, and the Arts, 6, 59

Cork Critters, 7, 74

Crystal Springs Rhododendron Gardens, OR, 42

di Rosa Preserve, 13, 59

Double-fold straight grain binding, 79

Dragon Dumplings with Shrimp, 70

Duckhorn Vineyard, 59

Duck Walk Vineyard, 59

Elk Cove Vineyard, 36

Emerald Valley (Barbara Baker/Jeri Boe), 36–39

Empty Spools Seminars, 8

Fabrications, 23

Fair Play, CA, 27

Fallert, Caryl Bryer, 22

Fenestra Winery, 10

Ferrari-Carano Vineyards and Winery, 5

Finish, of wine, 66

Fitzpatrick Winery & Lodge, 7, 27

Flora Springs Label Quilt (Catherine Comyns), 20

Flowers for Mommie (Vicki Chambers), 13

Flowers, three-dimensional, 30–31

Forest Star (Linda Glantz), 63

Fusible appliqué, 33, 36, 74

Fusible bias tape, appliqué with, 23, 25

Galante Vineyard, 8

Good Harbor Vineyards, 46

Got a Lot of Sunshine in My Heart (Anni Donohue), 13

Grahm, Randall, 6

Grand Traverse, MI, 46

Grape, gathered, 54

Grapes I (Babette Grunwald), 58

Grapes IV, Grapes V (Babette Grunwald), 57

Grapes Nouveau (Barbara Baker/Jeri Boe), 42–45

Grapevine Wreath (Carolyn Bachsmith), 41

Grape Wreath Medallion (Nancy Busby), 14–19

Grasier Vineyards, 5

Half-square triangles, 29

Hand Maden, 8

Hargrave, Harriet, 28

Healdsburg, CA, 23

Heller/Durney Vineyards, 8, 59

Heller, Toby, 8

Hermann, MS, 72

Hess Collection, 59

Hip Chicks Do Wine, 42

Hop Kiln Winery, 23

Ice wine, 46

In the Arbor (Phyllis Hoffman), 52–56

In Vino Veritas (Babette Grunwald), 57

Jewels in the Vineyard at Dawn (Mary Ellen Parsons), 8

Jimtown Store, 23

Joseph Swan Vineyards, 23

Joulian Vineyards, 8

Kent, Darcie, 12

Kenwood Vineyards, 59

King Estate Winery, 36

Lake Michigan, 46

La Vendange (Kathy Davie), 40

Layering, quilt, 78

Leelenau Peninsula, MI, 46

Les Bourgeois Vineyards Label Quilt (Cyndy Lyle Rymer), 21

Lewis, Laurie, 42

Livermore Valley, CA, 4, 10

Livermore Valley Cellars, 10

Machine appliqué using fusible web, 79

Martha's Vin Rosé (Mary Lou Fahrni), 62

Matanzas Creek, 5

McKim, Ruby, 27

Messina Hof Wine Cellars, 59

Miller, Jessel, 22

Mondavi, Robert, 7

Monterey, CA, 8

Mumm of Napa Valley, 59

Napa Valley, CA, 4, 5, 13

Navarro Vineyards, 6

Neely, Renée, 42

North Fork, Long Island, New York, 41

O'Brien, Tricia, 70

October (Sondra Townsend Donabed), 58

Old Mission Peninsula, MI, 46

Olive oil, 5

Oregon, 33, 36

Pacific Grove, CA, 8

Parsonage Winery, 8

Pasteur, Louis, 52

Phillips, Cheryl, 13

Pinot Noir (Jan Rashid), 32

Pinot Noir (Barbara Baker/Jeri Boe), 33–35

Portland, OR, 42

Pressing, 78

Private Collection (Jan Smiley), 59–61

Prosser, WA, 57

Puttin' on the Glitz Table Topper, 67–68

Quiltmaker (quiltshop), 13

Raftshol Vineyard, 46

Road to California: Fair Play Fun, 7, 27–31

Robert Talbott Vineyards, 8

Rust Ridge Winery Label Quilt (Anni Donohue), 21

Seam allowances, 78

Serendipitous Vineyard (Cyndy Lyle Rymer), 22

Shadow Boxes with a Twist, 72–73

Sheppard, Richard, 23

Simplest Wine Country Dessert, 71

Sisters Outdoor Quilt Show, 36

Sonoma, CA, 4

Stella de Uva (Tam Ravenhill), 13

Stem stitches, 54

Stenciling, 47–48

Stitchin' Post, 36

Strip piecing, 36, 42, 44

Sutter Home Inn, CA, 18

Tasting wine, components of, 65–66

Thomas Coyne Winery, 28

Through the Grapevine (Joyce Engels Lytle), 7, 10–12

Trapunto, 16–17

Wente Vineyards, 10

WillaKenzie Estate, 36

Wine charms, making, 64

Wine labels, as art, 20–21

Wine labels, fabric, 49

Wine tasting, hosting, 64–66, 70–71

Woodward Canyon Winery, 59

About the Authors

Cyndy Lyle Rymer & Jennifer Rounds
Photo by Jan Grigsby

Cyndy Lyle Rymer began to take quilting classes in 1972, and she hopes her first quilts never surface. Since that time, she has made many quilts and finally feels like she might be "getting it." Since moving to California from Hopkinton, Massachusetts (home of the starting line for the Boston Marathon and many good friends), her quilting tastes have changed dramatically. Cyndy got her feet wet as a production editor at Prentice-Hall/Simon & Schuster, New Jersey, and is now a development editor for C&T, where she enjoys working with all the fabulous and inspiring authors, as well as with her co-workers. She was the creator and editor of *Quilts for Guys*, co-editor of *Bouquet of Quilts*, and compilation editor for *Shoreline Quilts*, all recent releases of C&T. She appreciates the fact that her entire family supports her quilting habit, and have not tired of pizza—yet!

Jennifer Rounds jumped into quilting feet first without tools or significant knowledge of the craft. In her first quilt, she used old album covers as templates and pieced heavy chintz florals. She acquired a rotary cutter and a straight edge by her second quilt, but she used her kitchen cutting board instead of a rotary mat. Jennifer has become far more sophisticated since and much kinder to her equipment. She makes quilts by commission and includes a major Northern California hospital among her clientele. Jennifer writes the "Feature Teacher" column for *The Quilter* magazine, co-edited *A Bouquet of Quilts*, and is developing additional titles for C&T Publishing. Outside of quilting, Jennifer works as a freelance writer and handles domestic policy for her husband, two teenage sons, and family dog.